This book
belongs to

_____

and

_____

a couple after
God's own heart

A Couple After God's Own Heart

JIM & ELIZABETH GEORGE

HARVEST HOUSE PUBLISHERS

EUGENE, OREGON

A Word of Thanks

Every book in print is evidence of a multitude of miracles. For us, a few of our miracles during the writing and editing of *A Couple After God's Own Heart* came in the form of editors par excellence. From our hearts we wish to thank God for Steve Miller, senior editor, and Kathleen Kerr, associate senior editor, for invaluable help and guidance coupled with their energetic encouragement throughout the writing of this book. These two seasoned editors and friends, along with LaRae Weikert, Barb Sherrill, and Betty Fletcher, cheered us every step of the way to getting this book into your hands. Thank you, one and all. And thank you, Bob Hawkins, and all your capable staff at Harvest House Publishers, for your unwavering support of us and our books.

With thanksgiving to our Lord,
Jim and Elizabeth George

Contents

Before You Begin

Asked to define the game of golf, one man said cynically, "Golf is a good walk spoiled." Maybe the person who made this statement had just finished a bad round. Or maybe he hadn't been trying very hard, or he didn't feel golf was important enough to make it worthwhile to try to improve his game.

Whatever the case, this person's statement is clearly a negative assessment of the sport. And unfortunately, there are a growing number of people today who spout this same kind of attitude toward marriage. What's sad is that God intended that the joining together of a man and woman would bring the greatest human happiness known to mankind.

To any thinking person, it's obvious that it is the bad golfer—not the game of golf itself—that is at fault. In the same way, it isn't the divine institution of marriage that's at fault, but the husband and wife who are the "bad golfers"—the bad partners—when it comes to their marital issues.

Now, getting back to our golfer—if he was wholly committed to the game, he would gladly make every effort to become the best golfer he could be. Then he would enjoy the game a lot more. In the same way, if a husband and wife are both wholeheartedly committed to their marriage, they will make every sacrifice and do whatever is necessary to keep their relationship healthy, growing, and fulfilling.

Many people want a good marriage, but oftentimes they don't want to do what it takes to become the best spouse possible and work through life issues as they pop up along the way. It's easier (or so they think) to get a new partner! Or to simply go through the motions, doing only the absolute minimum that might be expected in maintaining a marriage relationship.

This book is written to and for couples who want to work at improving their marriages—couples who desire to follow God (together!) and reap the lifetime of blessings that are sure to be theirs. We—Jim and Elizabeth—as a couple are hoping and praying that, as you begin to make your way through the pages of this book (and hopefully also the *Couple After God's Own Heart Interactive Workbook*) you will commit to building a marriage that lasts. We don't have to tell you that no marriage is perfect, but we pray that you, along with us, are progressing toward being a couple after God's own heart.

Oh, and one final note: This book has been a challenge to write—a refreshing challenge! It's true that we have a lot we can share with you to help your marriage mend, grow, and improve—whichever is needed. But we too are still on the marriage journey ourselves. We still have to apologize and say, "I'm sorry, babe." We can still get upset with each other. And, believe us, we still have times when complete stupidity marks our actions toward each other.

And here's a challenge for you: As you read along, whose voice will you hear throughout this book? Will it be Jim's voice or Elizabeth's? Will we qualify our words by prompting, "Jim speaking," or "Hi, it's me, Elizabeth, who's now writing"? We decided (an example of teamwork!) to write as one voice because we want you, as husband and wife, to read this book together—as a couple.

As you make your way through this book, you may not even notice when one of us leaves off and the other begins. (And isn't that the way it should be in a good marriage?) Oh, there'll be some places where it's obvious Jim is talking to husbands and Elizabeth chimes in for wives, and vice versa. But on the whole, our desire is for this to serve as a seamless treatment of that wonderful—and demanding—institution called marriage. The two of you will enjoy journeying together through the lives of key couples in the Bible. You will also benefit from the lessons in God's Word that can help you to grow toward a richer, more intimate love for one another. And blessing upon blessings, you will grow closer together as you share the devotional in the second half of this book, which was created just for you as a couple after God's own heart.

Before you begin chapter 1, here are a couple of sobering thoughts for you to ponder:

> —In 1788, Edward Gibbon, the English historian and author, finished the sixth and final volume of the now-classic *History of the Decline and Fall of the Roman Empire.* He offered several basic reasons for the collapse of the Roman Empire, and one of them was the decrease in the dignity and sanctity of home and marriage, which included the problem of a rapidly growing divorce rate. That reason is strikingly applicable to our society today.

> —In AD 30, Jesus, the Son of God and God in human flesh, said, "[God] who made them at the beginning made them male and female, and said, 'For this reason a man shall leave his father and mother and be joined to his wife, and the two shall become one flesh'…Therefore what God has joined together, let not man separate" (Matthew 19:4-6).

Gibbons is right—for when marriages fall apart, it affects more than just the couple. It affects the immediate family and others beyond. The repercussions are felt in the church, the community, and even in society as a whole.

Which is why you as a husband and wife need to take Jesus' mandate in Matthew 19:4-6 seriously. God's design for marriage has always been one man and one woman, together, for the rest of their lives. This is God's intent, for good reason: A strong and intimate marriage relationship is a perpetual fountain of joy and blessing to both the couple and everyone around them.

With that in mind, let's look to the life examples of key marriages in the Bible, and discover what it takes to be a couple after God's own heart!

PART ONE

Following God Together

1

Adam and Eve

The Original Couple After God's Own Heart

Therefore a man shall leave his father and mother
and be joined to his wife,
and they shall become one flesh.
GENESIS 2:24

It was another perfect day in paradise, and Adam was busying himself at the far end of the garden. Today his to-do list called for naming the animals. "Let's see now," he said to himself as he stretched. "What should I call these two creatures? They look similar—except one has stripes and the other has spots."

Adam knew he was talking out loud, but it obviously didn't matter since no other person existed on the whole planet except Eve. *And, by the way,* he thought to himself, *I wonder where Eve is? She's usually close by, but I don't see her. Hmmm.*

Meanwhile, off in a brilliant field of multicolored flowers, Adam's wife, the exquisite Eve, was leisurely making her way toward the center of the garden. As she strolled along, delighting in the beauty of the garden and the variety of its wildlife, she occasionally became overwhelmed by the pleasure of her surroundings. She couldn't help stopping often to linger and stroke and inhale the different assortment of flowers, each with its own unique features and fragrance.

Knowing Adam was off naming the animals, Eve was quite startled by the pleasant voice of one of the creatures entwined around that one "special" tree in the garden. Propelled by curiosity, she walked slowly toward the voice, fascinated that this animal could speak. Mesmerized by the creature's voice, Eve couldn't help but listen.

The beautiful being casually said to the woman, "Has God indeed said, 'You shall not eat of every tree of the garden'?"

Eve responded to the creature, saying, "We may eat the fruit of the trees of the garden; but of the fruit of the tree which is in the midst of the garden, God has said, 'You shall not eat it, nor shall you touch it, lest you die.'"

Then the creature questioned these restrictions and God's motives for the restraints: "You will not surely die. For God knows that in the day you eat of it your eyes will be opened, and you will be like God, knowing good and evil" (Genesis 3:1-5).

As Eve listened, suddenly God's limitations seemed a bit harsh and didn't make so much sense. And besides that, the fruit did look delicious. Maybe she had misunderstood the restrictions. And, since the creature had so confidently stated that only good could come from the fruit, Eve shrugged her shoulders and concluded, "Why not?" And she ate.

What's Going On?

Do you ever try to imagine what life in the perfection of the Garden of Eden might have been like? We have, and our retelling of Adam and Eve's experiences in the garden may reflect a little of our imaginings. We do, however, know there's no way to describe perfection…but we can't help but try to picture it. But the subtlety of the creature (referred to as "the serpent") and the innocence of Eve could easily have happened in a similar manner.

The outcome of this drama and its disastrous results are firmly and forever detailed in the Bible and imprinted on our present-day lives and marriages. With the importance of this encounter that altered the history of mankind in mind, let's take a closer look at some specifics from the Bible and see how all this unfolded for the world's first couple.

The Command (Genesis 2:16-17)

Before God created Eve, Adam was alone in the Garden of Eden. It was at this time that God gave Adam a specific, do-don't command: "The LORD God commanded the man, saying, 'Of every tree of the garden you may freely eat; but of the tree of the knowledge of good and evil you shall not eat, for in the day that you eat of it you shall surely die'" (Genesis 2:16-17).

Could it be any clearer? God very explicitly laid down the law for living in the garden. Do—eat anything you want and eat as much as you like. Don't—eat from just this one tree, the tree of the knowledge of good and evil. God even told Adam the consequence of disregarding His command—you will die.

Ever gracious and generous, God gave Adam unlimited freedom to eat from any and all trees—except one. Talk about a Texas all-you-can-eat feast! With all that was available, there shouldn't have been any problems, right?

Wrong! Read on...

The Creation (Genesis 2:18-22)

God knew of Adam's loneliness, and He also knew the perfect solution:

> It is not good that man should be alone; I will make
> him a helper comparable to him...But for Adam there
> was not found a helper comparable to him.

> And the LORD God caused a deep sleep to fall on
> Adam, and he slept; and He took one of his ribs, and
> closed up the flesh in its place. Then the rib which
> the LORD God had taken from man He made into
> a woman, and He brought her to the man (Genesis
> 2:18-22).

Notice the time line. Adam received his instructions from God
(make that he received his *command* from God) when he had no
wife. Then, some time later, Eve was created. She was created from
Adam's body—from one of his ribs. And she was brought forth
for a purpose—to help Adam. She was to be his intimate companion, his friend, and his Number One helper and encourager (never
mind there was no one else to help him!).

Nowhere in the Bible is there any indication that God repeated
His instruction concerning the prohibition of eating from the tree
of the knowledge of good and evil to Eve. Whatever she would
know and needed to know, we must assume would have to come
from her husband, Adam, for he was the keeper of this information.

The Creature (Genesis 3:1)

"Now the serpent was more cunning than any beast of the field
which the LORD God had made" (Genesis 3:1).

Where did this come from? When God finished His creation
of all things, He declared all His handiwork "good." So what
happened? The answer most scholars give is that we must assume
that an evil force was speaking through this creature.

The Confrontation (Genesis 3:1)

In the idyllic sin-free surroundings of the Garden of Eden, Eve
had no experience with evil or cunning, with liars and deceivers.
Yet she found herself face-to-face with a talking beast, the serpent,
who said, "Has God indeed said, 'You shall not eat of every tree
of the garden'?"

Temptation often comes in disguise, quite unexpectedly. Speaking through the serpent, Satan began his attack of sly, veiled slander and lies against God. Evidently Eve was not alarmed by the snake because she was apparently drawn in by a familiar presence. God had created life and order. But Satan now brought death and chaos.

The Conspiracy (Genesis 3:4-5)

Throughout the Bible God's people are warned against false teachers and prophets. And here—in only the third chapter of the first book of the Bible!—we witness the first skewing and twisting and manipulation of God's Word: "Then the serpent said to the woman, 'You will not surely die. For God knows that in the day you eat of it your eyes will be opened, and you will be like God, knowing good and evil.'"

Satan's strategy was brilliant—and as deadly as an assault rifle. He cast doubt on God's Word ("Has God indeed said...?"), and on His goodness and motives ("God knows that in the day you eat of it your eyes will be opened, and you will be like God"). As a master orator, for his grand finale, Satan succinctly and blatantly contradicted God, who had warned of death as a consequence of eating the fruit. Satan cried out instead, "You will not surely die."

The Confusion (Genesis 3:2-3)

There is a now-classic book on marriage entitled *Communication: Key to Your Marriage.*[1] Yes, communication *is* key, and do we ever see this truth—and the results of a failure to communicate—in the confusion we now hear in Eve's words as she takes on the devil. We scream, "Don't do it!" and shake our heads as we hear Eve say to the serpent, "We may eat the fruit of the trees of the garden; but of the fruit of the tree which is in the midst of the garden, God has said, 'You shall not eat it, nor shall you touch it, lest you die.'"

What?! Now where did that come from? Surely Adam and Eve had often—maybe even daily—passed by that "special" tree.

Surely they had multiple opportunities to talk about the tree and its significance, about what God had cautioned regarding its fruit. Surely they had discussed and recalled that God had given Adam (not Eve) the prohibition regarding the tree of the knowledge of good and evil. The instruction was a mere four words long—"You shall not eat." (Good grief, even a kid would get this!)

Either Adam did a poor job of communicating this unbelievably simple warning to Eve, or she chose to forget—or dismiss—parts of God's command. In fact, she created what she obviously thought was a new-and-improved version, adding, "...nor shall you touch it, lest you die." That was not in God's original command. Whatever happened, and whoever was at fault, Eve minimized their privilege to eat freely in the garden, added the prohibition about touching the fruit, and downgraded the penalty of God's original command from "You will die" to "You might die."

It's obvious that, when it came to resisting Satan, Eve was unequipped and unskilled at fending off his attacks.

The Consequences (Genesis 3:1-19)

Eve was deceived by the snake and disobeyed God—she ate the forbidden fruit. That was Step 1 of her slide into sin...followed by Step 2: Eve offered the fruit to Adam, who ate with full knowledge that his action was wrong (1 Timothy 2:14).

We don't know if Eve knew she was wrong and presented the fruit to Adam because sinners love company. Or maybe because she didn't die right away when she ate and the fruit tasted so delectable she wanted to share it with her beloved husband. Whatever the reason, she gave it to her husband, and he ate. Did they experience instant gratification? No. Instead, they experienced instant awareness of sin as the eyes of both of them were opened (Genesis 3:6-7).

And their downward slide continued. Step 3: Adam and Eve tried to cover their sin and shame by making clothing and hiding themselves from God's presence (verses 7-8). Then in a face-to-face question-and-answer session with God, they slipped easily to Step 4: Adam blamed Eve and God ("The woman whom You gave to be with me, she gave me of the tree") for his wrongs, while Eve blamed the creature ("The serpent deceived me") (verses 12-13).

The Extent of Their Fall

Check out the fallout from sin as we wrap up this tragic tale. Talk about a horror story—and it's one that still affects all people—and couples—today!

- Shame as the two sinners realized their nakedness and sought to cover themselves by making clothes (verse 7).

- Separation from close fellowship with God (verse 8).

- Strife as each blamed someone else for what happened (verses 12-13).

- Sacrilege as Adam blamed God (verse 12).

- Sacrifice as God shed the blood of an innocent animal—the first blood spilled and the first animal to die in the perfect, sinless world He had created—to provide tunics of skin to clothe two sinners (verse 21).

- Suffering when they were banished from the garden into a now imperfect, sin-filled world, which included an ultimate physical death later in time (verses 16-19).

Putting It All Together

There is so much in the lives and marriage of Adam and Eve that you and your spouse will never be able to relate to. No other couple was created by God out of dust and out of bone. And no other couple had the chance to live in a perfect world. And no other couple ever walked and talked with God—literally!

But all couples can certainly identify with Adam and Eve's

failure—to one another and to God. We can recall bad choices we made that had lasting consequences on our marriage, our children, our finances, our health, and our job. We can point to something we did or didn't do that changed the course of our life forever.

Keep this perspective in mind as you check out some of the life lessons you can take away from "The Original Couple After God's Own Heart."

• Lessons for Wives from Eve •

1. *Remember your purpose.* I know, I know—you've already got a long list of responsibilities and job assignments from God. But a key role is named by God in Genesis 2:18: "It is not good that man should be alone; I will make him a helper comparable to him." Eve's first and Number One role—and the purpose for her creation—was to complement, complete, and fulfill Adam and to be a helper to him—to be, in a word, a "wife." I especially love the translation that reads, "I will provide a partner for him" (NEB).

A year after I became a Christian I sat down and wrote out some goals for my life. I started out with pen in hand and wondered, *Well, who am I?* What had changed since I'd accepted Christ? The answer was both simple and profound, and it eventually became my life's mission statement: "I am a Christian woman, wife, and mom."

With that statement I knew the aim of my life. As I approach each day, I don't have to wonder what my purpose is. It's to bring glory to God as a woman who knows Christ, to love my husband, and to love my children (Titus 2:4-5).

Your husband is Number One. He's the most important person in your life—right after God Himself! How about a Post-It note for your heart? "Today I am my husband's helper." And it never hurts to put those Post-Its in a few other places...like in your Bible, on the cover of your prayer journal, in the kitchen, and on your car's dashboard so you can be reminded of your purpose as you travel back home from work, school, church, or errands.

2. *Always ask.* You can certainly see from Eve's mother-of-all-blunders how quickly things can go downhill when we as wives fail to check in with our husbands. So, when in doubt, check it out. Even if there's no doubt, it's still a good thing to run your issues by your guy.

The Bible teaches that the head of every man is Christ, and the head of the woman is the man (1 Corinthians 11:3). A husband is responsible for his wife. So ask your husband when you are unsure. I can't count the number of times I've screamed at myself, "Elizabeth, don't be an Eve! Find out what Jim thinks." I've learned (like Eve did—the hard way) to ask first, act second. Of course, our goal as a couple is to have the same mind. And I admit, things go very well when I ask Jim, "Honey, what do you think I should do?" and he gives me an answer that I like. But I've also learned to listen to his answers and his reasons, and to respect his thinking even when I don't like or agree with his answers.

Whatever you're facing or wondering about—how to discipline the kids, whether or not to lay out a certain amount of money for some item, or if you should go back to school, get a job, join the choir at church—ask. Your aim is to be partners through life, and as partners, you want to move forward in step, as a unified force. As the proverb states, "Two are better than one, because they have a good reward for their labor. For if they fall, one will lift up his companion" (Ecclesiastes 4:9-10).

3. *Know your enemy—and how to fight back.* Temptation is a count-on-it-every-day occurrence. So prepare yourself for it. Don't get caught off guard. Gear up for the onslaught and the battle. How? Begin your day in God's Word. Let His truths ground you,

focus your thoughts, steady you, empower you, polish up your perspective, and help you get your head screwed on so you're thinking and responding according to God's Word. If Eve had God's command firmly—and accurately—fixed in her mind and heart, if she had memorized it and repeated it every day, imagine how differently the results from her encounter with the enemy might have turned out.

When you watch a tennis match, you'll notice the players are always on their toes, bouncing their weight from foot to foot, shifting their racket from side to side, hand to hand, ever moving and on guard, eyes riveted forward, just watching and waiting for the ball to blast toward them. Well, that's got to be you. Temptation will blast toward you today...and every day. It's as predictable as the sunrise. Carry that image with you as you enter each day with all its unknowns, its challenges, and its temptations.

And here's something else you can count on: "Your adversary the devil walks about like a roaring lion, seeking whom he may devour" (1 Peter 5:8). And how exactly do you fight such a powerful enemy? "Be sober, be vigilant....resist him, steadfast in the faith" (verses 8-9).

Oh, and while you're at it, don't tempt your husband! Don't be an Eve. Two wrongs never make a right. Eve ate, and that was wrong. And asking Adam to eat was also wrong. I repeat, don't tempt your husband.

4. *Forgive your spouse.* There's no question that Adam and Eve had some serious forgiving to do. They had both failed—and failed each other. Worse than that, they had failed God. And they had even blamed each other—and God—for their failures. But thank God that in providing a covering for their sins and wrongs, He provided the example of forgiving others.

After your husband really fails, and after he really *really* fails, you are to forgive him. There can be no "going on" without pardoning your partner. The New Testament tells us we are to forgive one another, even as God in Christ forgave you (Ephesians 4:32). As a Christian, you have experienced God's forgiveness of your sin. Therefore you can—and are commanded to—extend forgiveness to others, beginning right in your own marriage.

You and your hubby can talk about your issues later, make plans for how to avoid or handle similar situations in the future, and take responsibility for his and her individual contributions that led to failure. But the first step to continuing on in your marriage is to forgive each other. And what if he doesn't or won't forgive you? Doesn't matter—God still expects you to forgive him.

So be quick to say, "I'm sorry" to your husband. Be determined not to blame your mate. Confess your part and your failure to God and ask His forgiveness. And be equally as quick to accept God's forgiveness and rise up and move forward.

5. *Go on.* As terrible and devastating as Adam and Eve's failure was—a 10 on the Richter scale—my favorite part is that they went on. In reality, there was no choice—they were ejected by God from their home in the Garden of Eden. But they still had each other. I like to picture this forlorn-but-forgiven couple acknowledging that the way back into the garden was truly shut forever, and then Adam reaching down and entwining Eve's hand with his as they looked into each other's eyes, then boldly facing forward and taking their first step into the unknown—together.

Both Jim and I grew up in Oklahoma. In Ponca City is the Pioneer Woman statue—a tribute to the women who gallantly packed up all their earthly possessions and, whether on horseback or in a wagon, left their homes and headed West alongside their men. Relentlessly they pushed westward, where they made new homes on the lands their husbands gained. This monument was created to honor the grit and spirit these frontier women possessed as they endured harsh conditions and forged a new life.

When I think of such conditions and the fortitude it took for the pioneers to leave the familiar and step into the unknown, I think of Adam and Eve. This brave twosome stepped out of a sinless, perfect paradise…into a world filled with hardship. God cursed the ground and told Adam, "In toil you shall eat of it all the days of your life…In the sweat of your face you shall eat bread till you return to the ground" (Genesis 3:17,19). And to Eve God said, "In pain you shall bring forth children" (verse 16). This couple suffered the consequences of their sin, but they went on. They moved ahead—together.

The same must be true of you and your husband. You're both going to fail God and you're going to fail each other—that's just a fact. But God has provided all that you need as a wife to go on to wherever God—and your husband—leads you. God extends His forgiveness. His grace is sufficient. His mercies are new every morning. And He is with you—always. This means you can go on.

• Lessons for Husbands from Adam •

1. *Remember your purpose.* (This is the same for you as it is for your wife!) God gave Adam dominion (Genesis 1:27-28). As the "firstborn" of God's human creations, Adam was responsible for everything. God entrusted not only the animals to Adam's care and oversight, but also his wife, Eve. Adam was assigned to be the leader. And, to add the full dimension to that role, you, like Adam, are also to be the spiritual leader in your marriage.

Spiritual leadership has been a husband's mandate from the time of creation itself. God gave Adam personal and specific instructions about God's dos and don'ts of the garden. Adam's job was to pass that information along to Eve and to make sure they as a couple followed God's directions to the letter. Somewhere along the line this information was either improperly communicated to Eve or somehow misunderstood by her. Whatever happened, ultimately it was Adam's responsibility, as the spiritual head of the marriage, to make sure his wife got it right.

It's God's design for the husband to be the spiritual leader of the marriage and family. He is supposed to lead his wife and children in Bible reading and the study of God's Word. But somehow in our modern society, many husbands have abdicated this role and no longer lead their families spiritually. What's one easy way to turn things around? Take the initiative and make sure your family regularly attends a Bible-teaching church. You can also encourage your wife to take part in a Bible study. You don't need a theological degree to lead—all you need is to remember your purpose: Lead your family in the ways of the Lord! And if you are not that man right now, ask someone to mentor you and help you live up to your calling, to your purpose.

2. *Be available.* Adam was there…but he wasn't there. Sure, he had a job to do, but he either didn't see what was happening between Eve and the serpent, or he saw them talking and chose not to get involved. After all, he was doing what God had asked him to do! As men, we are generally by nature nomadic creatures. We love to hike, go on adventures, travel, and we have no problem moving from place to place. Women, by contrast, tend to prefer roots and routine. They like everything to be in its place, all neat and orderly with as few ripples as possible. Adam, as our prototype, was out naming the animals, while Eve was left alone to wander in the garden.

How can you be available to your wife if you or both of you are working at jobs and separated for part of the day—or longer periods of time? One vital thing you can do as a leader is develop some basic ground rules for being there for her. Maybe you call her a couple times a day to see how she's doing. That's one way Elizabeth and I keep in touch during our crazy days. On more than one occasion, that timely phone call helped us clear up a problem, answer a concern, discuss how to proceed on a project or responsibility, or how to handle a "kid issue." Or, best of all, it gave us another opportunity to say, "I love you." It's a little thing, but connecting really does make a difference. As one phone company says, "Reach out and touch someone"—and that someone would be your wife.

3. *Be protective.* We're back again to what it means to be a leader. Sometimes as guys we use our role as leader par excellence to "delegate" things onto our wives.

Actually, *dumping* may be the more appropriate term. After all, in general, most wives are usually great at multitasking. Just look at the way they juggle the home, the kids, their jobs and responsibilities, their ministries at church, and both their parents and ours! So we conclude, Why not ask her to take the car into the repair shop? Or, hey, she's pretty good at math. Why not let her take on responsibility for the family finances and make sure the bills are paid on time?

The list of tasks we husbands can delegate could go on and on, and unfortunately, sometimes it does! Our wives are so competent that we are more than happy to let them carry burdens we could shoulder ourselves. (Of course, if your wife is great at math and enjoys budgeting, you could let her do this while you take on something else around the house.) Face the facts: Your wife already has a lot on her plate, with her roles as a wife and mom and home manager and perhaps a worker as well. Your job is to protect her so she can continue to do her best in her primary roles. She's not your assistant; she's your wife.

4. *Be an encourager.* Sin brought a curse and judgment into the world and into the lives of Adam and Eve. Can you imagine how Eve must have felt after the bottom dropped out of her 100 percent perfect and beautiful life? She wasn't malicious in her desires. She didn't set out to willfully disobey God. No, she was deceived, and

her fall into temptation brought about terrible consequences—the worst! Her home was destroyed. Her relationship with God was altered, not to mention her relationship with her husband. She had to feel lower than that snake's belly.

All of the above occurred, and in no way does that mean Adam was not also at fault. There's an Italian proverb that says, "When a wife sins the husband is never innocent." But still, that didn't make things any easier for Eve. This is where Adam came to the rescue, and where you as a husband can help your wife.

After Adam got over blaming his wife, we read that he and Eve moved on. "And Adam called his wife's name Eve, because she was the mother of all living" (Genesis 3:20). The name *Eve* means "life," or "life producer." What a positive statement, especially after having just received God's death sentence—Eve, the mother of all life! The name Adam gave his wife wasn't one that would brand her, or mar her, or serve as a forever reminder of failure. No, it was a statement that exalted her into a position of honor and respect. It gave her a future and a hope.

Many books report that a large number of women suffer from low self-esteem and a lack of confidence and self-worth. I often travel with Elizabeth to her women's conferences, and she and I occasionally end up giving counsel to some of the attendees. I think because Elizabeth and I have learned to work together as a team, the women see this teamwork in us and yearn for it in their marriages. With tears in their eyes, they describe their husband's attitude as exhibiting self-centeredness or a lack of tenderness. Through pain they will say something like, "I just wish my husband would whisper 'I love you' once in a while. He's sure able to complain when things go wrong. Why can't he show a little appreciation when things go well, which they do most of the time?"

Here's a quick start for you. Right now, stop reading and tell you wife, "I love you." If you're not together at this moment, call, email, or text her. Then splurge when you see her and tell her you

appreciate her. You know you do. So let her know she's the greatest thing that's ever happened to you, because she is!

Building a Marriage that Lasts

There are three basic elements needed to build a structure that
lasts: a foundation, a blueprint, and tools.

In Adam and Eve we can't miss the foundation—love. Love for
God and the love of God, along with love for each other, enabled
this brave couple to face a dark and problem-filled future.

They also possessed the divine blueprint for marriage. God had
laid out the specific roles for the husband and wife: Adam was to
lead, and Eve was to be his helper, his complement, the one who
completed him.

And, as the first couple ever left the safety and perfection of the
Garden of Eden, they departed with the tools needed for building
a marriage that lasts: forgiveness and hope. They carried in their
hearts God's promise given in Genesis 3:15 that Eve's "seed"—Jesus
Christ—would one day crush, destroy, and defeat Satan.

As you work on building your marriage—and as you as a couple
face your trials—remember these words: "Each new day is another
chapter in the unfolding promise of deliverance and life." [2]

Where Are You on the Countdown to Communication?

Level Five—Talking trivia. This is safe, superficial, and little more than a warm-up for real conversation: "How's the weather outside?" "How are you doing?" "Just fine, thanks. And you?" "Fine." "Hey, can you hand me that newspaper?"

Level Four—Reporting facts about others. This level is somewhat more interesting, but still there is little risk of self-exposure. "I noticed that John and Mary bought a new car." "How was work today?"

Level Three—Sharing ideas and impressions. Here is where real communication begins. You no longer play it safe, but are willing to take risks or reveal your thoughts and opinions, which can be accepted or criticized or rejected. "I think we ought to make that move. What do you think about this…?"

Level Two—Unveiling feelings and emotions. At this level you reveal not only your thoughts but your heart. At "gut level" you disclose what's most important to you by communicating your heartfelt convictions and what moves you. "I love you." Or "My faith is real to me because…"

Level One—Being completely honest, open, and vulnerable. This is the most mature level of sharing, where marriage partners become best friends as they share their deepest joys, fears, and struggles. "If I could do anything in world, I would like to…" "I have this sin in my life…" "My biggest struggle or fear is when…" "My greatest dream is…" [3]

2

Abraham and Sarah

Then Abram took Sarai his wife…
and all their possessions that they had gathered,
and the people whom they had acquired in Haran,
and they departed.

GENESIS 12:5

"Home is where the heart is." Your heart is the seat of your emotions and feelings. So, if your heart feels comfortable and at home in Dry Gulch, Arizona, it's going to be hard to get you to leave such a place, in spite of how others might view your choice. It's home at least to you and thousands of rattlesnakes!

Let's take a little time-travel trip back to 2100 BC, to a place called Ur, about 185 miles southeast of modern-day Baghdad. Back then Ur was a wealthy and sophisticated city, and that's where the couple taking center stage in this chapter lived—the soon-to-be-patriarch Abraham and his wife, Sarah, whose name meant "princess."

Sarah loved the energy of Ur. Located on the banks of the great Euphrates River, the city of Ur was the site of constant comings and goings of ships and barges as they bore goods from faraway places. Being from a prosperous family, Sarah could afford to buy many of the exotic items that came to Ur. And, of course, she loved being near her family. Ur had been the family home for untold generations.

Yes, life was good! But as Abraham entered their home one evening, all that was about to change.

"Have you ever thought about leaving Ur?" Abraham blurted out breathlessly, as if he had been running for some distance—and as if there was no good way to bring up this topic! Sarah looked up from her loom and didn't even pause before she replied with a gracious "No" (instead of the loud "No way!" she was tempted to shriek at him).

Abraham went on. "You're not going to believe what happened in the fields this morning."

"Now, Abe, let's not play twenty questions," Sarah smiled and teased, hoping to move this discussion along. "What happened?"

"I talked to God. Not the wooden gods we've been worshiping, but the true God. The *one* true God! He appeared to me today, and told me to depart from my relatives and go to a place He would show me. Sarah, I couldn't wait to tell you about it!"

This definitely got Sarah's attention. "Now let me get this straight. Some kind of god I've never heard of is asking you to pack up and leave Ur? Did I hear you correctly?"

"Yes! That's exactly what He said," Abraham nodded.

After a long pause, Sarah stammered, "Are you out of your mind? No one, and I mean *no* one, leaves Ur, especially to go to some mysterious place, to Whoknowswhere! This has got to be the craziest thing I've ever heard!"

This was going to be an incredible test on Abraham and Sarah's marriage. They would have to pull out all of their 2100 BC communication skills to reach some sort of agreement on this one! But we do know how this story ends. Abraham and Sarah—and at least part of their family—did pack up and move away from Ur and toward God. And eventually, because of their faith in the Lord, Sarah and Abraham arrived at God's destination—the center of His will for them.

Packing Up and Leaving

This sounds like a pretty crazy story, doesn't it? Probably right about #1 on "A Woman's List of Worst Nightmares"! But couples down through the centuries have made similar monumental decisions without knowing what lay ahead.

Elizabeth and I have made dramatic decisions too. For many years we were an unequally yoked couple—I was a Christian and Elizabeth wasn't. One Thursday, after eight years of marriage, Elizabeth came to Christ. By the following Monday I had sent off an application to apply to a local seminary to train for the ministry. It had been a life-changing weekend, for sure.

As Elizabeth tells the story, "There I was, less than a week old in the Lord. I had just purchased my first Bible on Sunday, and now I was going to be a pastor's wife? All I can say is, I'm so glad I didn't know at the time that, in order to go to seminary, Jim would have to leave his very nice job, and we would have to sell our very nice house and most of our very nice possessions to finance his training. Talk about being a modern-day Sarah!"

But there's more…just as there always is in Christ! After I (Jim) had been in the ministry for several years, I went on a ministry trip to Asia with our church's pastor of missions. While we were traveling and ministering our way through parts of Asia, the two of us mapped out a grand scheme for missions and leadership training for that part of the world.

After three long, intense weeks of travel and ministry, I was finally on my way home. When I landed in Hawaii to change airplanes, I called Elizabeth. Because I had no access to phone connections while I was in Korea, the Philippines, Singapore, and India, this was my first opportunity to phone home.

What I could have said: "Hey, honey, how are you? How are the girls? I've missed you and can't wait to see you!"

What I actually said: "Hey, how would you like to move to Singapore?"

Elizabeth's response was the same as it had been with so many of my other crazy ideas: "Sure!" Then she asked, "Where's Singapore?"

Thus began a whirlwind of activity as we packed up and left home for a new life of faith and ministry in Singapore (which, by the way, Elizabeth now knows is located in the South China Sea, 85 miles north of the equator, roughly halfway between India and Australia).

What's Going On?

Meet Abraham and Sarah (Genesis 11:29-30). As we encounter this couple, there is no drum roll or drawn-out introduction. Unlike the miracles and dramatics that preceded God's creation of Adam and Eve, we simply read a mini-history and genealogy of Abraham and Sarah (who were named Abram and Sarai before God changed their names)...and off we go!

> Now Terah lived seventy years, and begot Abram, Nahor, and Haran...Haran begot Lot. And Haran died before his father Terah in his native land, in Ur of the Chaldeans. Then Abram and Nahor took wives: the name of Abram's wife was Sarai...But Sarai was barren; she had no child (verses 26-30).

While our introduction to this couple is brief, the story of Abraham and Sarah and their glowing faith spreads across 13 chapters in Genesis, the largest amount of space given to any of the couples in the Bible.

God's Command (Genesis 12:1)

God gave Abraham an initial command: "Get out of your country, from your family and from your father's house, to a land that I will show you."

No pressure, right?

Abraham was from Ur of the Chaldeans, among the most advanced cities of its time, majestically situated along the lush banks of the Euphrates River. Ur was situated in what is called the Fertile Crescent, a region so named because of two large rivers at its heart, the Euphrates and the Tigris. These rivers brought trade and produced abundant crops due to the rivers' natural overflow and man-made irrigation systems. From this opulent urban center, which at the time would probably have ranked high on the "Most Desirable Places to Live" list, Abraham and his clan moved to the land of Canaan.

Which was quite a shift in real estate! Canaan couldn't have been more opposite the metropolis of Ur. The dry desert where Abraham would pitch his tents would make for rather sparse grazing for his massive herds of sheep and goats.

Regardless, Abraham did as the Lord instructed. God had told him to get out—to leave his country, his family, and his father's house. God was shutting the door to Abraham's past ties and connections and calling him to turn his life in a completely new direction. He didn't promise it would be easy. He just said *go*.

A Promise for the Future (Genesis 12:2-3)

With the door slammed on the past and the future uncertain, God gave Abraham a comforting promise and assurance:

> I will make you a great nation; I will bless you and make your name great; and you shall be a blessing. I will bless those who bless you, and I will curse him who curses you; and in you all the families of the earth shall be blessed.

God commanded...and Abraham responded. With a heart of faith, a heart willing to obey, and a promise to hold onto, Abram departed (verse 4) and stepped into his unknown future.

Off our couple Abraham and Sarah went, following after God's own heart. Imagine the heart-wrenching good-byes! Moving is never easy or free of difficult emotions. So how did Sarah respond to Abraham's wishes? From the silence of Scripture and what Peter later wrote about her, Sarah was wholehearted in her trust in God and in Abraham, even calling her husband "lord" (1 Peter 3:6).

A Couple in Crisis (Genesis 11:30)

The first record we have of Sarah is a description of her physical condition: "Sarai was barren; she had no child." In today's culture, this condition is difficult and often a source of personal pain. However, most couples in this kind of dilemma can adjust their goals and lifestyle expectations and move on without too much stigma. And because many couples today choose not to have children, a childless home isn't all that unusual.

But not so in 2100 BC. Barrenness was a really big deal! So much so that it was even a justifiable reason for a man to divorce his wife. We don't know how long Abraham and Sarah had been married when they began migrating to Canaan, but we do know that Abraham was 75 years old when God told him to leave Ur (Genesis 12:4). So Abraham and Sarah had probably been married for decades. Her barrenness was not a recent thing. They had lived with this "cultural curse" day and night for a very long time.

And what made her condition more painful and confusing was the fact that God had promised Abraham that he would become a great nation. To become a great nation, he had to have some children, right? As the years—and decades—dragged by, Abraham and Sarah definitely became a couple in crisis!

Beauty and the Beast (Genesis 12:10-20)

Abraham and Sarah had acted on God's command to leave Ur and, as a couple—as partners in faith—they had boldly followed after God's own heart. Then *bam*! They had barely arrived at their destination when they were faced with a famine. What a shock after having lived for so long in the Euphrates River valley. Famine? Their homeland knew no such thing!

What were they to do? The logical next step to take would have been to go to a place where they could find food. So without even consulting God, they headed for Egypt. If Abraham had taken the time to look to God, and had waited on the Lord to speak to him, then he would have been assured that he was in God's will and didn't need to make alternate plans.

But there is no record that Abraham, "the friend of God" (James 2:23), the man God spoke to multiple times, reached out to the Lord for guidance in this matter. We'll never know if God would have sent this husband and wife to Egypt or not. Rather, they went totally on their own, which means Abraham was making his own decisions and following his own advice. Here's what being out of the will of God looks like: Because Sarah was extremely beautiful and desirable—even at age 65—Abraham feared for his life in pagan Egyptian society. So he came up with a plan to protect himself:

> He said to Sarai his wife, "Indeed, I know that you are a woman of beautiful countenance. Therefore it will happen, when the Egyptians see you, that they will say, 'This is his wife'; and they will kill me, but they will let you live. Please say you are my sister, that it may be well with me for your sake, and that I may live because of you" (Genesis 12:11-13).

What happened? Right on cue, when the couple arrived in Egypt, Pharaoh took one look at the gorgeous Sarah and, after being told that Sarah was Abraham's sister, put her into his harem. While this was actually a half-truth—Sarah was Abraham's half-sister by the same father but by different mothers—it was also a half-lie because they lived together as man and wife. In spite of Abraham's beastly cowardice and lack of faith in God's protection,

God was patient—and powerful. He protected Sarah and sent great plagues upon Pharaoh and his house (verse 17). To Sarah's credit, nothing is mentioned in the Bible about how she responded to Abraham's deceptive actions.

Trouble in the Tent (Genesis 16)

Fast forward about one decade. For ten years Sarah and Abraham lived with God's promise of an heir…but Sarah was still barren. We can be sure Sarah cared—deeply—that there was no heir. We can be sure she yearned—deeply—to hold a baby. And we know she gave their couple-problem a lot of thought because eventually she hatched a big plan for getting an heir. Plan A had been a baby from Abraham and Sarah. When that didn't seem to be working, Sarah came up with Plan B: She would offer her maid, Hagar, to Abraham to impregnate, yet the child would be his and Sarah's. She even pulled God into her argument: "Sarai said to Abram, 'See now, the LORD has restrained me from bearing children. Please, go in to my maid; perhaps I shall obtain children by her.' And Abram heeded the voice of Sarai" (verse 2).

God had promised Abraham a son, but, at least in Sarah's thinking, He hadn't specified that the child would come from Sarah. So why not follow the culturally accepted practice of the day and use a substitute to conceive and give birth to a child? Once again, there is no record that Sarah or Abraham—partners in faith—consulted with God, who had led them out of Ur and given them the promise of children.

Abraham's troubles started when he listened to his wife, Sarah. Now, realize this account in the Bible is *not* teaching that a wife cannot make suggestions to her husband, or share her thoughts and ideas. And it is *not* saying it's wrong for a husband to listen to his wife and put her ideas into action. In fact, many times a wife's advice is the best help a husband can receive. After all, your wife is your life partner and knows you better than anyone else does.

But Abraham made two mistakes. First, he assumed Sarah's

arguments were valid. But what about the fact she had added God into the mix? Maybe Sarah thought that strengthened her arguments, but it certainly didn't sanctify or give authority to the suggestion. It's like your spouse saying, "God told me we should do this or that." And second, Abraham assumed Sarah's offer was based on purely unselfish motives—that she was truly trying to help the cause, help Abraham move forward as a family head, and maybe even help God out with fulfilling His promise.

The events that transpired after the birth of Hagar's son, Ishmael, prove that Sarah's true spirit was less than gracious and loving. Sarah became mean and bitter and treated Hagar cruelly. Then later, after Sarah at last gave birth to a son, Isaac, she asked Abraham to send Hagar and Ishmael away into the desert. Abraham once again listened to his wife. This time, however, God confirmed Sarah's suggestion, saying to Abraham, "Do not let it be displeasing in your sight because of the lad or because of your bondwoman. Whatever Sarah has said to you, listen to her voice; for in Isaac your seed shall be called" (Genesis 21:12). We can be sure it was a sad, miserable, heartbreaking day for Abraham when he sent his son Ishmael away.

When there is a crisis, don't make the same mistake Abraham and Sarah did. Before you take action, pray! And when there is trouble in your marriage and your family, pray!

Portraits in the Hall of Faith (Hebrews 11)

In spite of their issues as a couple, Abraham and Sarah were a man and a woman of faith—a couple of faith, partners in faith— a couple after God's own heart. Beyond their story in Genesis, this dynamic duo is mentioned for their faith in God in four New Testament books.[4] How did Abraham and Sarah exhibit their trust in the Almighty?

By faith. "Abraham obeyed when he was called to go out to the place which he would receive as an inheritance" (Hebrews 11:8). When God told Abraham to perform a sign of God's covenant with him, he obeyed by circumcising all males in his house

(Genesis 17:22-23). Later, God told Abraham to sacrifice his only son—and Abraham obeyed by heading to Mount Moriah with his son (Genesis 22:1-19). Abraham's modus operandi when dealing with God was to obey quickly and completely, with no hesitation.

> *By faith*...Abraham trusted God. God told Abraham he would become a great nation, and even though he was childless at the time—and for a long time afterward—he believed in the Lord, and it was accounted to him for righteousness (Genesis 15:6).
>
> *By faith*...Sarah trusted her husband to lead her, "whose daughters you are if you do good and are not afraid with any terror" (1 Peter 3:6).
>
> *By faith*...Sarah received strength to conceive in her old age, and "she judged [God] faithful who had promised" (Hebrews 11:11).

Are you growing in God as a couple? Are you partners in faith? God is not looking for perfection, only progression. And each new day holds an opportunity for the two of you to make progress. If you are like most couples, you are not where you want to be, right? So the question you might want to ask God and each other is this: "How can we develop our faith as a couple and grow more spiritually mature as Christians?"

Though Abraham and Sarah had times when they disobeyed God, He still watched over and cared for them because ultimately they would turn their trust to Him. If you want to follow in their steps, the first way to grow a stronger Christian marriage is by listening to God—learning and knowing what He says in the Bible. If you take the time to count, you'll discover at least nine times when God conversed with Abraham or Sarah. And God is still speaking to His people and His couples through His Word, which is available to you today and every day.

To live up to your potential as a couple after God's own heart and grow deeper roots of faith, you need to spend some time each day in God's Word. Try reading the same chapter in the Bible and then talking about it. Look for a book of devotions for couples and take turns reading it out loud. Pick a few favorite verses or promises from the Bible and memorize them together. Aim at keeping a steady, daily stream of God's rich, nourishing Word coming in to fuel your spiritual growth as partners in faith.

Abraham and Sarah are both mentioned in Hebrews 11, which is often referred to as God's "Hall of Faith." As you observe them traveling together for decades and listening to God and following hard after Him—even when they didn't know where they were going—you see their faith in action. This is what faith in your marriage will look like when you look to God and His Word, listen to what He has to say to you, and then follow Him with all your heart as you travel through life together.

Putting It All Together

One thing you can definitely appreciate about the saga of Sarah and Abraham is that you get to examine a couple that finished the marriage marathon, a couple whose portraits hang forever in God's Hall of Faith. You are allowed to travel right alongside them through their thick-and-thin, better-and-worse, day-in-day-out challenges. You witness their problems, watch how they handled—or mishandled—their trials, and learn from the outcomes. You see a couple that is committed to God and to each other wade through problem after problem, fail one another and God (more than once!), and still weather every storm and come out of each test…together.

• Lessons for Wives from Sarah •

1. *Follow your man.* Jim and I attended a missions conference that became memorable and life-changing because of what a woman shared with us. This lady's husband was gung ho for missions and

gave her a card like the one he had signed that consisted of four A's. Beside each A was a check box. The four A's stood for Anything, Anywhere, Anytime, at Any cost. It took her husband under 30 seconds to check off all four A's, sign and date his card, and turn to his wife and say, "Hey, honey, here's yours!" But she froze and absolutely could not sign her card. She carried that card around for at least six months before she was finally able to check the four A's and sign the card. Did they end up on a mission field? No. But were they willing to follow after God's heart as a couple? Yes! Anything, anywhere, anytime, at any cost.

When I think of Sarah following Abraham, I can't help but think about those four A's. That's how I want to follow Jim, trusting God to lead me through my husband. Sure, a husband will make mistakes in leadership. What husband doesn't? But God asks my husband to lead (that's Jim's role), and He asks me to follow (that's my role).

This doesn't rule out communication, the give-and-take of information, the waiting, praying, and asking stages of decision-making. I think of responding to Jim's leadership as a sandwich—two slices of bread with lots of food items in between. The two slices of bread are "Sure!" and "Sure!" And the items between the bread slices? That's where I get to ask, "Okay, when would we do this? And how would we pay for this?" And if the issue is super serious, I ask, "Is there a godly man at church you can talk to about this?"

Try it. Go easy. Take your time. Above all, stay positive and calm. And offer up an abundance of prayers. Focus on the goal of following your man.

2. *Beware of your great ideas.* Sarah is not alone in this "beware" category! As you'll soon see, Rachel—and already Eve—also won awards in this uncoveted-award category. We don't know exactly what happened, but one day Sarah just snapped and out

of nowhere—in spite of all the repeated promises from God Himself—she had the "greatest" of all great ideas: "I'll get Abraham to have a baby with my maid!" Nothing but trouble came from the birth of Ishmael—trouble that has lasted more than 4000 years (in the form of the ongoing conflict between the Arabs and Jews).

When you have a great idea, don't do anything until you have followed a few fundamental steps of wisdom:

1) Stop—don't do anything.

2) Wait—only fools rush in.

3) Pray—for God's leading.

4) Search the Scriptures—for what God says about it.

5) Seek counsel—from wise people.

Then run it by your husband instead of making an outright announcement or demanding your way. Remember your goal—to be a partner to your husband.

3. *Be a team player.* In Genesis 18, a miracle occurred at Abraham and Sarah's tent. Three strangers showed up—but these were no ordinary strangers (verses 1-2). Needless to say, our partners in faith went into action. Abraham began giving orders. While Sarah rushed to make bread, he ran to the herd and selected a calf for the meal. At last this husband-wife team put dinner on the table for their three guests, who happened to be divine: the Lord and two angels!

You've probably heard that "too many cooks in the kitchen" leads to all kinds of trouble. But Team Abraham and Sarah did a great job. They worked together and pulled off a meal for their surprise guests.

Do your best to work with your husband on projects. Ask him how you can help, and include him whenever he wants to help you. Slide down into slow gear. Put on some music. Enjoy being together. Talk about your day or your dreams. Be a team player. These can be some really sweet times—times that will create precious memories.

4. *Learn to live without.* Some women live without a husband—either as a single, a widow, or a woman married to a man whose job often takes him away from home, even for long periods of time. Some women live without the money for basic necessities. And some women live without a real home. Sarah got a taste of a quasi-homeless lifestyle as she lived like a nomad, moving regularly. We know many missionaries who live their days in a crude "house" or even a handmade hut in the wilds of a jungle. Many of these couples and families live without conveniences that are firmly fixed on our can't-live-without lists—a television, car, bathroom, electric appliances.

Sarah, however, lived without a child! She went for decades wanting, wondering, and watching for a baby—a baby that God Himself promised to her and Abraham. She had the promise of a child, spoken from the lips of God. But her discontent led her to make a serious mistake. In her impatience, she connived to gain a child through a union of her husband and one of her servants. The result? Ishmael's descendants became the Arab nations, and the hostility between Arabs and Jews continues to this day.

5. *Focus on long-term faith.* Your faith in God is there to carry you through the long haul of life. We are blessed in Sarah to witness many seasons of a marriage. Yes, we read about some of her blunders and slipups—and one of them (setting up her husband and her maid) was monumental. But when God looked over her life, He chose to list her name among the giants of the faith!

Do whatever you need to do to strengthen your trust in God. Every time you read your Bible, you expand your faith as you learn more about God and His promises. Every time you pray, you are demonstrating faith. Every time you obey God—even when you don't understand—you are living by faith. God will carry you through every trial you will ever encounter as you run your personal faith marathon. My life verse gives a clear focus on the long race of life and how to successfully run it: "One thing I do, forgetting those things which are behind and reaching forward to those things which are ahead, I press toward the goal for the prize of the upward call of God in Christ Jesus" (Philippians 3:13-14).

• Lessons for Husbands from Abraham •

Abraham was a man of contradictions. He was a great and wealthy nomadic chieftain in his day. He was a skilled warrior. He was well-respected in the regions where he pitched his tents. But he made some bad decisions when it came to his marriage. So hang on to your hat! Abraham can teach you and me where to focus our attention…and what to avoid when it comes to our wives.

1. *Love your wife through thick and thin.* Abraham and Sarah had a big problem, yet he never seemed to be concerned about Sarah's barrenness. He never seemed to make an issue of it. He presents husbands with a firm challenge—we are to love our wives unconditionally. This is also the message to husbands from the New Testament, where Paul tells husbands to love their wives as Christ loved His church (Ephesians 5:25). When you married, you vowed to love your wife "for better or worse, in sickness and health," etc. When you face difficult circumstances, including physical challenges, you are to redouble your efforts and reinforce your love for your wife. Like Abraham, love and care about your wife, no matter what.

2. *Be consistent with your leadership.* Abraham wasn't perfect. He made plenty of mistakes. For starters, he failed to consult with God

on several key decisions and really messed up. He was passive at key periods in his marriage, such as when he was in Egypt (where he put Sarah at risk by saying she was his sister), and when he listened to Sarah's scheme and allowed Hagar to be the mother of his son Ishmael. Yet at other times he showed great leadership both with his family and his neighbors. This should give you hope in your own leadership. God has placed you as the leader in your marriage, so be sure to ask Him for the strength, wisdom, and resolve to be consistent.

3. *Openly worship God.* Abraham worshipped openly—and passionately. Although Abraham started out as a pagan, God, in His grace, did a work in Abraham's heart and life. What did this former pagan's life look like after God's makeover? He talked to God. He built altars to the Lord. He gave tithes. He listened to God. And he obeyed God.

Has God done a work in your life? You too were once a pagan, a sinner. But just as God loved Abraham and worked in his life, He also wants to work in yours. "God demonstrates His own love toward us, in that while we were still sinners, Christ died for us" (Romans 5:8). If God has worked in transforming your life, are there any of Abraham's spiritual activities that are beyond your abilities? I think you'll agree there aren't. So purpose to faithfully follow Abraham's example and lead your wife and family in spiritual pursuits.

4. *Diligently manage your resources.* There is nothing in the Bible that says you must be poor financially. In fact, the Bible exalts hard work and thrift, and points to such management as being rewarded by God's blessings. Abraham was never obsessed or lazy with riches, even though he was a wealthy man. But he was faithful to manage his possessions carefully. Today it's easy for couples

to chase after money, to sell their souls for a big house, fine cars or boats, fancy vacations…and the list goes on and on.

Because money is such a big—and daily—issue in marriage, here are a few things to consider as a couple:

- First, evaluate your hearts, individually and as a couple. Seek contentment. Make every endeavor to follow the apostle Paul's motto: "I have learned in whatever state I am, to be content" (Philippians 4:11).

- Second, determine what you need, not what you want. It's amazing during a financial recession or depression how little we decide we can live with and how much we can do without. This should be our attitude at all times.

- Third, if you are in serious debt, eliminate credit card spending as much as possible and pay cash for your purchases. It's too easy to flash "plastic money"—and you *really* pay for it later! Also, you'll spend less when you pay with cash because you generally have less cash with you, and you're hyper-aware of every "real" dollar you fork out.

- Fourth, but definitely not last, give or tithe a portion of every paycheck. For example, Abraham gave ten percent of the spoils from a victory over marauding bandits to Melchizedek, "the priest of God Most High" (Genesis 14:18).

As the man and husband of your household, you are responsible for the way your family's income is managed. Be faithful with this stewardship. And enroll your wife's help in controlling expenses. Set "couple goals" regarding your finances—what and where you should give, how much savings you should have on hand, what your household budget should look like. If you work on this together, you just may avoid the Number One culprit on the Things Couples Argue About Most list—money!

5. *Strengthen your faith.* Abraham was a man of faith. In fact, one man wrote a book entitled *Abraham, God's Man of Faith.* [5] From the very beginning of God's recount of Abraham's life, we see clearly that Abraham trusted God. He held onto and lived by the promises of God. They moved him to leave his homeland and family, and they motivated him to keep going year after year.

Abraham's faith served as a model for the apostle Paul's whole argument regarding faith in Romans 4. And the famous Protestant reformer Martin Luther based much of his conviction on God's establishment of Abraham as a pattern of faith. What a great epitaph this would be for your life:

> Here lies _____[your name]_____,
> a man who trusted God,
> a man of faith.

Fellow husband, follow the admonitions given in Proverbs 3:5-6 as you love and lead your wife and family. When you do, your faith will be strengthened as you see God point you in the right direction: "Trust in the LORD with all your heart, and lean not on your own understanding; in all your ways acknowledge Him, and He shall direct your paths."

Building a Marriage that Lasts

The life studies of Abraham and Sarah, a couple after God's own heart, comprise an extraordinary portrait! No other marriage in the Bible is given as much space. In the 13 chapters that detail their lives up until Sarah's death, we get a glimpse of the epic tale of their love, their trials, their partnership, and their adventures. Let's look at the three basic elements needed to build a marriage that lasts.

What was the *foundation* of their marriage—and their lives? There can be no doubt it was faith. Abraham, the husband, was a man of faith, and Sarah, the wife, was a woman of faith—God's perfect combination! They possessed strong individual trust in God, which made them partners in faith.

And they followed God's *blueprint* for their lives. What God said, they did. Like master builders—whether of an edifice or a marriage—they followed the specs and regulations set down by God. They had faith in Him and in His plans for them.

And the *tools* Abraham and Sarah used to build a marriage worthy to be mentioned in God's Hall of Faith? First, we see their heavy use of and reliance on the promises of God. We can only imagine the many discussions Abraham and Sarah must have had about the fact that they had no heir. And we can also imagine them continually and constantly reminding each other of God's sure promise. We see patience as a tool for trusting and living for God. They waited and waited…and waited for a child.

As you work on building your marriage, no matter what circumstances slam you, or how ridiculously stupid your mistakes are, or how much you must forgive each other, or how tough it gets to trust God and wait patiently on Him, pull out these words spoken by the Lord, face-to-face with Abraham, when He repeated His promise of a son through Sarah: "Is anything too hard for the LORD?" (Genesis 18:14).

The answer? No, of course not.

3

Isaac and Rebekah

A Marriage Made in Heaven

The LORD God of heaven...
will send His angel before you,
and you shall take a wife
for my son from there.

GENESIS 24:7

Cue the music. Heavy on the strings. Bring in soaring melody that tugs on your heart! The movie industry has nothing over the love story you are about to read in this chapter. The story of Isaac's marriage to Rebekah not only illustrates the way marriages were arranged in ancient times, but is also a seriously romantic love story. And there is no doubt theirs was a love match! Here's how this marriage "made in heaven" came to be.

By the time Sarah, the mother of Isaac, died at age 127, Isaac, an only child and the child of Abraham and Sarah's old age, was about 37 years old. Isaac didn't live in town, or just down the street, or across town. No, Isaac lived in a tent near his two very aged parents. For all of his 37 years, Isaac had watched his father and mother live in love. In fact, by age 37, his parents had lived together as a couple after God's own heart for more than 50 years.

Based on the Bible record, it is obvious that Abraham and Sarah loved each other. And the strength of their relationship was evident even in death. Genesis 23:2 tells us "Sarah died in Kirjath Arba (that is, Hebron) in the land of Canaan, and Abraham came to mourn for Sarah and to weep for her." The great patriarch and staunch giant of faith, Abraham, was visibly and physically moved by the death of his longtime wife, and he wasn't afraid to show his emotions to his neighbors. We now get to see how Abraham's love is modeled in the next generation through Isaac, his son.

What's Going On?

A Father's Concern for His Son (Genesis 24:1-4)

This is not a book on parenting, but Abraham's actions provide an excellent example of how vital a parent's counsel can and should be when it comes to guiding their children toward a mate who will be a suitable lifelong match—especially from a spiritual standpoint. This can be one of the greatest roles parents fulfill with regard to helping their children get off on the right foot in dating or court-ing, and ultimately, in whom they marry.

After the death of Sarah, Abraham decided it was time for his son, Isaac, to find a wife. One thing was certain: Abraham did not want his son to marry a local Canaanite who did not know God. Therefore, he sent his most trusted servant, Eliezer, on a mission. Abraham assured Eliezer that God would lead the way and assist him in finding the perfect wife for his son.

Notice the confidence Abraham had in God as he assures and charges his servant: "The LORD God of heaven…will send His angel before you, and you shall take a wife for my son from there" (24:7). When Abraham sent Eliezer back to the land from where he came, he was doing his best to find a bride who believed in the one true God. As he explained to Eliezer, "Swear by the LORD, the God of heaven and the God of the earth, that you will not take a wife for my son from the daughters of the Canaanites, among whom I dwell; but you shall go to my country and to my family, and take a wife for my son Isaac" (24:3-4).

A Marriage Made in Heaven (Genesis 24:5-62)

Abraham's most trusted servant's mission was to go back to Abraham's relatives in Mesopotamia several hundred miles away, and from there find a wife for his son. And he did as he was instructed. When the servant arrived in the area of Abraham's birth, he prayed:

> "O LORD God of my master Abraham, please give me success this day, and show kindness to my master Abraham. Behold, here I stand by the well of water, and the daughters of the men of the city are coming out to draw water. Now let it be that the young woman to whom I say, 'Please let down your pitcher that I may drink,' and she says, 'Drink, and I will also give your camels a drink'—let her be the one You have appointed for Your servant Isaac. And by this I will know that You have shown kindness to my master."
> And it happened, before he had finished speaking, that behold, Rebekah, who was born to Bethuel, son of Milcah, the wife of Nahor, Abraham's brother, came out with her pitcher on her shoulder (24:12-15).

As you read this story, you may be like many who apply some sort of "fairy tale" status to this account. A prayer is uttered. A sign is asked. An answer is received. What a story! Abraham's servant believed with all his heart that this young woman named Rebekah was just the girl for Isaac: She met the very expectation he had sought in his prayer to God. As you read the story you also can't help but observe how this match was orchestrated by God. But can you believe that your marriage was also made in heaven?

If you have just had an argument with your spouse, you might be wondering! Or, as you remember where and how you met, maybe you're not too proud of it. You may wonder if perhaps God was not involved.

In the past, Elizabeth and I had times when we wondered, "Were we really meant to be married to each other?" That's because we were what the Bible labels "unequally yoked" (2 Corinthians 6:14). In other words, I (Jim) was a Christian and Elizabeth was not. I had been a Christian from an early age but got off track in my spiritual life after leaving home to attend college.

After eight years of marriage, which added up to eight years of doing just about everything wrong as a couple, Elizabeth came to Christ. Immediately we started going to a Bible-teaching church and learning what it means to be a couple after God's own heart.

Regardless of what brought you and your spouse together, how and where you met, and what the circumstances were when you married, God was involved. Marriage, in God's eyes, is permanent. Moses wrote, "Therefore a man shall leave his father and mother and be joined to his wife, and they shall become one flesh" (2:24). And later in the New Testament Jesus provided this additional aspect of how God views *all* marriages, whether Christian or non-Christian: "Therefore what God has joined together, let not man separate" (Mark 10:9). Marriage is ordained by God and once a couple is married, it becomes a match made in heaven. Regardless of how it got started, it becomes a binding union.

Many couples lose sight of the fact that God views marriage as binding. You can't let any issues, problems, or speed bumps get in the way of the vows you made. As a couple, you are obligated by God to make your marriage work.

Maybe you were married as unbelievers. Or maybe you are on your second or third marriage. Or maybe a sexual indiscretion caused you to get married. Regardless of the details, here you are today—a couple, married to each other. Whatever the circumstances, you must see your present situation now as God's design. And, as a Christian couple, you must now see your marriage as sanctioned and blessed by God. It is to be permanent. You cannot redo the past—it's over. Yes, there may be regrets and consequences, but today, in this marriage, God wants you to make it work for His glory and your joy.

A Man Loves a Woman (Genesis 24:61-67)

What kind of relationship did Isaac have with Rebekah? Genesis 24:67 tells us, "He loved her." And, like his father, Abraham, Isaac showed visible love. This was an emotional love, and later Isaac is seen "caressing his wife Rebekah" (26:8 NASB), or showing a physical intimacy as well.

Love. It is an often-discussed topic in the Bible. Husbands are told to "love your wives, just as Christ also loved the church." They are to "love their own wives as their own bodies." And a husband is to "love his own wife even as himself" (Ephesians 5:25,28,33). A man's love for his wife is to be sacrificial, even to the point of gladly giving up his life if it means protecting his wife.

Love is action, not just saying the words, "I love you." The proof of your love will be seen in how you treat your wife. Do you honor her with a simple little thing like opening doors for her? Helping her in and out of the car? Helping her around the house, with the kids, with paying the bills? You get the picture!

We hope you're not like the man whose wife of 15 years cried out during a counseling session, "He never tells me he loves me anymore!" In startled disbelief the man responded in his own defense, "Well, I told her I loved her when we got married, and it still stands!"

A husband's love for his wife is to be practiced on an ongoing basis. When the apostle Paul wrote, "Husbands, love your wives" in

Ephesians 5:25, he went on to say this love was to be like Christ's love for the church. As we all know, Christ's love for the church is ongoing and unending. In fact, He showed love to the point of self-sacrifice—He gave His life for us. Likewise, husbands are to show an ongoing, unending, and self-sacrificial love for their wives.

A Fairy Tale with a Problem (Genesis 25:19-21)

Marriage is often described as a long-term roller-coaster ride. There are ups and downs. During their first few years of marriage, the only real problem the blissful couple had to face was the death of Abraham, which had to be a great loss for both Isaac and Rebekah. But in the midst of their sorrow, God just kept right on blessing Isaac (verse 11).

But there was one issue that had to have caused concern. And it reared its head every single day, right in Isaac and Rebekah's home. Its name? Barrenness. After 20 years of marriage, Rebekah was still without children. Like Sarah before her, this was a big deal for Rebekah.

You'll be happy to know that Isaac rose to the test and did the best thing anyone can do in a tough, impossible-looking situation—he turned to God in prayer. And it appears that his was not a one-time prayer of "Oh, by the way, Lord, Rebekah is barren. Can You do something about it?" No, it seems that Isaac earnestly and continually pleaded with God—"Isaac pleaded with the LORD for his wife, because she was barren" (verse 21).

And the outcome? God answered with twins! (verses 21-22).

A Failure to Communicate (Genesis 25:21-34)

This isn't the first time we've encountered this problem. Brace yourself—as with Adam and Eve, Isaac and Rebekah are about to have their own problems with talking—or not talking!—to each other.

Here's the problem: Rebekah was barren. She and Isaac had been married for 20 years, and still no children. Isaac, being a loving, sensitive, and caring husband, prayed for his beloved wife to conceive. And God answered with a double blessing—twins. We can only imagine the joy this couple must have felt when they discovered Rebekah was pregnant.

Yet while the twins were still in her womb, they were already struggling with each other. Rebekah, being a first-time mother-to-be, wasn't sure what was going on. So she went to the Lord with her problem and inquired of Him. And God answered: "Two nations are in your womb, two peoples shall be separated from your body; one people shall be stronger than the other, and the older shall serve the younger" (25:23).

What's interesting here is that apparently God told this only to Rebekah. There is no record that God communicated this same information to Isaac. Nor do we see that Rebekah relayed this news to her husband. Wouldn't you think Rebekah would have fainted or screamed out loud, and then run to Isaac to share what God had said regarding their future sons—that the older would serve the younger, meaning that Esau would serve Jacob? But evidently Isaac didn't know, for years later, when it came time for Isaac to bestow the right of the firstborn on Esau, he ended up giving that right to Jacob.

A Family of Favorites (Genesis 25:24-28)

From the beginning, Isaac and Rebekah's twin boys struggled and were opposites in just about all categories—in character, manners, and habits. And each boy appealed to the personality of one of the parents. Before their sons were born, Isaac and Rebekah had centered all their love on each other. Yet as parenting became more of a focus in their lives, their love seems to have shifted and began to revolve around their children. The Bible says Isaac loved Esau, and Rebekah loved Jacob (verse 28).

What devastating words! And what a sad scene—a family unit made up of divided love, with each boy only half-loved. Could anything good possibly come from this kind of warped affection?

A Family Likeness (Genesis 26:1-11)

Earlier we mentioned that, according to the apostle Paul, a husband is to love his wife with a self-sacrificial love (Ephesians 5:25,28). Unfortunately, too often the opposite happens. Abraham, Isaac's father, had lied about his wife twice—to Pharaoh and Abimelech—saying that she was his sister. Why did he do this? "That it may be well with me" (12:13; see also 20:2). Abraham was more concerned about self-preservation than self-sacrifice.

And now we are presented with the legacy of Abraham's negative example in Isaac! There is again a famine in the land. But this time God specifically told Isaac not to go to Egypt. He promised that if Isaac stayed in the land, He would take care of him: "Do not go down to Egypt; live in the land of which I shall tell you. Dwell in this land, and I will be with you and bless you; for to you and your descendants I give all these lands, and I will perform the oath which I swore to Abraham your father" (26:2-3).

Isaac obeyed God and stayed right where he was. His home was smack-dab in the middle of land owned by the Philistines—a group of people who were going to give the Israelites some trouble in later years. Isaac wasn't sure about the character of these people…especially when it came to Rebekah. She was probably well into her sixties by this time, but she was still incredibly beautiful.

Unfortunately, Isaac's anxiety level ran too high. To protect himself against his imaginary fears, he took on a survival strategy similar to that of his dad. He lied about his relationship with Rebekah, telling the locals, "She is my sister" (verse 7). Isaac obeyed God with one decision—he stayed in the land—but failed to trust God and turned around and decided to lie about his wife. Again, self-preservation instead of self-sacrifice.

What happened to loving his wife enough to sacrifice his own life for her? And what could the awful consequences have been if the local men wanted his "sister" for themselves? And what of Rebekah's feelings—to be betrayed and let down by her own husband? Isaac definitely let God down, and just as definitely let Rebekah down. And he let down husbands through the ages who would have expected better from him, that he would set a strong example of what true love looks like in action.

A Dysfunctional Family in Action (Genesis 27:1–28:5)

We know that God told Rebekah that Esau (the firstborn) would serve Jacob (the secondborn). Again, it appears Isaac had no knowledge of this. When it came time for Isaac to bestow the right of the firstborn, he was set to give the blessing to Esau. It was the custom.

What happened? we wonder. Did Isaac not get the memo? Did Rebekah fail to tell her husband what God had said? Maybe Rebekah had told Isaac 20 years earlier, and Isaac forgot. Or maybe Isaac chose not to listen to what God had to say. After all, Esau was his favorite.

Whatever happened, Rebekah still has time to tell Isaac of God's earlier prediction. No matter what, Rebekah was faced with a dilemma. Would she trust God to do as He had said, or should she move in and try to "help God out" with what seemed to be a problem?

When it became obvious things weren't working out to Rebekah's liking, she went into high gear to manipulate her favorite son—Jacob—into the position of blessing. Talk about dysfunctional! A couple not sharing important messages and events. Parents showing favoritism. A spouse trying to deceive and manipulate a partner.

The endgame? Ultimately, Rebekah got what she wanted. Jacob did receive the blessing. But what a price she paid! She alienated her son, Esau. Out of anger, Esau arranged a marriage with a godless foreigner, knowing this would displease his parents. And out of anger, Esau made a vow to kill his brother. Jacob was forced to flee for his life, and Rebekah never saw her favorite son again. What a tragic turn of events! Her last recorded words in the Bible express great sorrow and regret: "I am weary of my life" (27:46).

Putting It All Together

How can a relationship begin so beautifully and end so badly? Isaac and Rebakah's marriage began as an answer to the earnest prayer of Abraham's trusted servant. Looking at the first half of their marriage, we would get the sense that Isaac and Rebekah's marriage was a match made in heaven. They loved each other and settled into a beautiful life together. The one problem we see is that for the first 20 years, Rebekah was childless. But Isaac pleaded with God for a child, and God responded by granting not one, but two children—twins!

By the time Jacob and Esau were born, it becomes evident that Isaac and Rebekah are drifting apart. Each has a favorite child. Their story ends with Rebekah helping her favored son, Jacob, deceive her husband and Jacob's father into giving Jacob the blessing of the firstborn, rather than to the rightful heir, Esau. The family was torn apart as Jacob was forced to run for his life, and Esau, in rebellion, married a woman from idolatrous neighbors. Such a tragic ending after a thrilling, hopeful beginning! But praise God that, in spite of this couple's shortcomings, He would find a way to weave even their mistakes into the fabric of a brighter future.

• Lessons for Wives from Rebekah •

1. *Character counts.* When Abraham's servant went looking for a wife for Isaac, he found every character quality he thought Isaac needed in Rebekah. As a young unmarried woman, probably in her teens, Rebekah was a "lady-in-waiting"—waiting to discover who her husband would be, waiting on marriage. So, while she waited, she devoted herself enthusiastically to doing her part for the family and taking care of her work.

Every day she went to the well to draw water for the family. But on one particular and special day, her life took a dramatic turn in a new direction. It all started with her willingness to serve others—more specifically, to serve the servant of Abraham. Eliezer asked God to lead him to a woman who was willing to serve others. Rebekah passed that test, but her service went beyond giving the tired man a drink. She volunteered, "Drink, and I will also give your camels a drink" (Genesis 24:14).

Think of Rebekah's long list of character qualities—qualities God applauded, qualities that help make you a great wife. She was a go-getter. A self-starter. Helpful. Compassionate. Observant. Energetic. A quick thinker. Clever. Reliable and responsible. Hospitable. She saw a need and met it. She was probably the life of the family. And there was probably a dust cloud following her as she raced from one activity to the next.

Lay your daily life as a wife beside this list. Take a self-test. Are you lacking in any of these qualities? Are you focusing your time and energies on your husband, home, and family—on serving others? Is there any one quality you need to pay special attention to today?

2. *Child-centered parenting can endanger your marriage and family.* When it came to her twin sons, Rebekah played favorites. In her household, Isaac loved Esau because he was a hunter and provided him with tasty food. And Rebekah loved Jacob because he loved to hang out in the kitchen and help his mom—he was a "momma's boy." Both Isaac's and Rebekah's partiality drove the boys to make poor choices that deepened their character flaws. Jacob became a trickster, and Esau grew into a wild rebel who married godless women and wanted to kill his brother.

When parents—one or both—favor any child over another, they cause friction and emotional pain. If your family relationships have turned sour, talk to your husband about it. Or ask a close Christian friend or counselor for help. Then ask God to supply you with His fruit of the Spirit, love, for each of your children. God's love is pure love, and it contains no partiality. With the Spirit's love, it is impossible to love one child more than another. Don't endanger or lose your family for lack of love when Christ has enough love for everyone!

What more can you do? Creating a prayer notebook with a page for each child will help ensure each child is at the forefront of your mind and heart. And on your husband's page, write down a reminder to pray fervently that he will love each of his children. Every child should have two parents who love him or her.

3. *Believe the promises of God.* At the end of the day, Rebekah did not trust God. Even though God spoke directly to her when she was having problems before the birth of her twins, Rebekah still failed to trust His word: "The LORD said to her: 'Two nations are in your womb, two peoples shall be separated from your body; one people will be stronger than the other, and the older shall serve the younger'" (Genesis 25:23).

Pretty clear, right? Yet, when the time came for Isaac to bless his firstborn son, Rebekah failed to trust God to fulfill His word. She doubted that God would or could intervene on Isaac's behalf, that God would make sure Isaac gave the blessing to Jacob and not Esau. As the time of blessing drew near, Rebekah panicked and took matters into her own hands, hatched a plan, and went into action to manipulate events so the birthright would go to Jacob, the younger. Rather than trusting in God's promise, standing back, and beholding God at work, she trusted in her own plan of deception.

A lack of faith in God cost Rebekah and her entire family dearly. She lost her precious son, Jacob, as he fled for his life. That was the last she ever saw of him—she died before he returned. And she lost her son Esau, as he left in anger to marry a heathen woman—an action that he knew would break her and Isaac's hearts.

Trust is essential in any relationship, and that's especially true of your relationship with God. Are you having a problem trusting God with some aspect of your marriage, or where your children are concerned? God's Word provides answers. Don't try to manipulate your life, or your husband's, or your children's. Trust God that He already has everything worked out for your good, your husband's good, and your children's good. Trust in His promise in Romans 8:28: "We know that all things work together for good to those who love God, to those who are the called according to His purpose."

And there are a few things you can do when you're afraid your husband is making a mistake. First and foremost, you can—and should—always speak to God about your concerns. Pour out your heart and your fears as you ask for divine wisdom.

You can also speak to your husband. Choose your words and timing carefully, and ask lots of questions rather than make accusations. He is your mate, your children's dad, and your best friend. You should be able to talk openly with him.

In the end, after all the praying, all the talking, and all the caring, you must then trust God to work out each situation, to work in your husband's heart, to work in your child's life—and to work in your heart.

4. *Review your role as a wife often.* No, make that daily! Rebekah was not a good helper. Maybe in the beginning she was, but in time she failed to fulfill this role. God gave Eve to Adam to be his helper. And Rebekah was given the same assignment—she was to help her husband. Everything started so well. After all, theirs was the marriage made in heaven!

But somewhere along the way, Rebekah stopped helping her husband and started hurting him, their marriage, their sons, and their family unity. She began pitting her wits against Isaac's plans to give Esau the birthright. A good helper and wife would have gone to her husband when she first received the news about the twins. A true helper would have shared the message from God and then prayed as He and Isaac worked out the details. A helpful wife would have done everything in her power to hold her marriage and family together rather than let them get into the convoluted mess Rebekah created—a mess that hurt everyone. Follow the model of the Proverbs 31 woman, the ideal wife:

> Who can find a virtuous wife?
> For her worth is far above rubies.
> The heart of her husband safely trusts her;
> So he will have no lack of gain.
> She does him good and not evil
> All the days of her life (31:10-12).

What to do? In the spiritual realm, pray. In your prayer notebook, create a page for you as a wife. List God's four roles for you on this page: Help, Submit, Respect, and Love. [6] Looking at these four roles every day and praying to live them will keep them fresh in your heart.

And practically? Constantly ask yourself, "Will this action, choice, or behavior help or hinder my husband?" Your goal? As the proverb above stated, "The heart of her husband safely trusts her...She does him good and not evil all the days of her life."

• Lessons for Husbands from Isaac •

1. *Gentleness is strength under control.* This quality speaks of an ability to stay calm, no matter what happens. Gentleness is also a sign of godliness, and is listed as a fruit of the Spirit in the New Testament (Galatians 5:23). A godly husband is to be a leader who is marked by gentleness and a calm manner. Isaac exemplified this quality—we could say he was a true gentleman, a gentle man.

We see this virtue in Isaac as he is meditating in a field along the caravan route leading to Canaan. This route brought Rebekah to where Isaac was walking and thinking. We see it again in his sensitivity to his wife's barrenness. Moved by her condition, he prayed for Rebekah's childlessness, and God answered his prayer (Genesis 25:21).

Humility is a noble and biblical quality every man should cultivate and possess. Most wives would love their husbands to show a little more gentleness and sensitivity to their needs and those of the children. Thinking, pondering, meditating, and praying are all aspects that signify a heart of humility.

However, this same quiet spirit can have its dark side. Like his father Abraham, Isaac asked his wife, Rebekah, to pretend they were brother and sister out of fear that he might be killed because of her beauty (26:7). Isaac's conduct provides a word of caution: A quiet spirit of meekness is noble until it becomes a passive spirit that fails to lead, fails to make decisions, fails to stand up for what is right, true, and godly, and, as in Isaac's case, fails to protect the honor and safety of your wife. Pursue the godly quality of gentleness, remembering that it is strength under control.

2. *Tap into the power of prayer.* Isaac was a special husband in two ways. He was, as Genesis 24:67 tells us, a husband who "loved" his wife. And Isaac prayed for his wife (25:21). Rebekah was barren for many years, a great concern for both of them as a couple. Isaac knew that only God could intervene and solve the problem.

Like Isaac, you need to be a husband who intercedes on behalf of your wife. This is a key role and responsibility you have as a Christian husband. Pray for her and all of her many responsibilities. Her needs and concerns should be a high priority for you as her husband, best friend, and leader. What a comforting and calming effect your prayers will have on your soul mate as she realizes that at least one person—you—is praying for her, that you are her very own prayer-warrior husband!

3. *Emotions are a good thing.* Maybe it was his godly quality of humility, or his gentleness, but Isaac definitely had a soft side. He wasn't afraid to show his emotions, and he freely expressed his love for Rebekah. Demonstrative love is easy and natural for newlyweds. Everything is a first-time experience, fresh and exciting.

But even after 20 years of marriage, Isaac still cared deeply for his Rebekah, and that care showed in his prayers for her to have a child. And later, after 35-40 years of marriage, when he and his family were threatened by famine and traveled to Gerar to survive (also the place where he lied, saying Rebekah was his sister), Isaac showed his love in a physical way. In fact, that was what blew the whistle on the lie he told the king about his relationship with Rebekah: "Abimelech king of the Philistines looked through a window, and saw, and there was Isaac, showing endearment to Rebekah his wife. Then Abimelech called Isaac and said, 'Quite obviously she is your wife'" (Genesis 26:7-9).

Having an emotional side is essential for a husband after God's own heart. It moves you to feel deeply, act strongly, and pray fervently. And it helps you follow God's command to live with your wife "with understanding, giving honor to the wife, as to the weaker vessel" (1 Peter 3:7). Being a man means you will probably never understand your wife completely. But as you pray for her, care for her, and make an effort to know her better, you'll be there for her. You'll be more aware of and sensitive to her needs. You'll be tuned in to her when her heart hurts or she's down physically or emotionally.

4. *Love needs direction.* In the world of physics, matter is never lost—it simply changes its state. Love is like matter: It isn't lost; it's only redirected. Isaac's love was directed full-on toward his wife Rebekah for at least the first 20 years of their marriage. Their love started out as a marriage made in heaven. But somehow it got redirected. After twins Jacob and Esau arrived and the newness and

glory of finally having children wore off, the parents' affections moved from full-out love and adoration...to a time of adjusting to an expanded family of four...to a cooling-off time of choosing sides against one another. Isaac redirected his love onto his favorite son, Esau, while Rebekah showered her love on Jacob. Somewhere in the rough seas of marriage, this couple drifted apart.

Your love as a husband is to be directed toward your wife—period. Your concern should always be, "Is my love fully aimed toward my wife?" A wise husband realizes that his marriage is a work in progress. This means you will need to do your part to keep it alive and vibrant. You can never think that your marriage has *arrived*, that you've reached the stage where bliss will reign in your relationship forever without any further effort on your part. Marriage is an open contract between you and your wife, and only death closes the contract.

Building a Marriage that Lasts

The love of a husband and wife is an incredible and wonderful mystery. The fire of your love will not sustain your marriage unless that fire is fed, stoked, stirred, and constantly tended. The more it is fueled, the greater its flame. Bless one another in your marriage. Don't complain that you don't have time to work on your marriage. Make the time, and you'll have a marriage made in heaven.

4

Jacob and Rachel

Jacob served seven years for Rachel,
and they seemed only a few days to him
because of the love he had for her.

GENESIS 29:20

When we last saw Jacob, about all we saw was the dust cloud behind his heels! He was running—running for his life. To save himself from the murderous wrath of his brother, Esau, he fled 400 miles through burning desert sands.

Why? Why would Jacob leave his childhood home? His parents—Isaac and Rebekah? His brother—his twin brother?

From the time Jacob was born, his childhood home had been one of division. One parent loved one son, and one parent loved the other. Tension and treachery and trickery came to a head when it was time for Isaac to bless the elder son—the firstborn twin, Esau—with the major portion of his inheritance and with the promise of God's continued favor.

But Rebekah wanted Jacob to get this blessing. She and Jacob had schemed together to deceive Isaac, and swindle her son Esau out of his rightful inheritance. The only solution to this family feud was for Rebekah's beloved Jacob to leave home to save his skin. And so he ran for his life. Because his brother had threatened to kill him, Jacob's parents sent him back to the home of his mother's roots, to Rebekah's people, to find a wife.

Jacob didn't get very far before he learned through a dream that God was going with him. Through his dream, God reaffirmed His covenant (initially made to Abraham) with Jacob and his family and vowed, "I am with you and will keep you wherever you go, and will bring you back to this land" (Genesis 28:15). This comforting, encouraging message came at just the right time as Jacob fled into an unknown future—homeless, penniless, and without a single friend.

When Jacob awoke, it was indeed a new day! His fears were replaced with a powerful promise for his future. Armed with God's personal assurance that He would be near, Jacob traveled the 400 sandy desert miles to Haran, the land of his mother's family. It was a long and lonely trip, but finally, *finally*, he spotted an oasis where shepherds were watering their flocks.

What happened next would make a great opening scene for a bestselling novel or movie. We will now see how the deceiver (for that is what Jacob's name means—a name he definitely lived up to) becomes the one deceived.

What's Going On?

Love at First Sight (Genesis 29:1-12)

At long last Jacob arrived at a watering hole near the hometown of his mother's family in Haran. Catching his breath after an arduous trek, he, a man on a mission, immediately inquired about his mother's family. His mom had carefully instructed him, "My son, obey my voice: arise, flee to my brother Laban in Haran. And stay with him a few days, until your brother's fury turns away...then I will send and bring you from there" (Genesis 27:43-45).

When Jacob asked the shepherds about his mother's family, he was given good news—his uncle Laban was indeed there, alive and in good health. In fact, his daughter, Rachel, was now approaching the well with the family's sheep. Jacob took one look at this Rachel...and he was hooked. Hopelessly. A stunning local beauty, Rachel was described as "beautiful of form and appearance" (29:17).

Jacob couldn't resist showing off. He ran over to the well and singlehandedly moved a stone away from the mouth of the well so the shepherds could water their flocks. He then told Rachel who he was and, in a fit of emotion, kissed her, and lifted up his voice and wept. From this point on Jacob's sole mission in life was to win Rachel as his wife. He then moved in with Laban and spent a month with his family, including his two daughters—the beautiful Rachel, and Leah, the elder sister.

A Dowry Is Set (Genesis 29:15-18)

Yes, Jacob was hooked—maybe a little *too* hooked. He was completely blown away by Rachel's beauty. There's certainly not anything wrong with "love at first sight," and this situation didn't involve the parents planning any kind of arranged marriage. But something crucial was missing: There is no record that Jacob consulted with God before committing to marrying the exquisite Rachel. With nothing to offer—no wealth or inheritance—his intense love for Rachel caused him to sell himself to Laban as a dowry for her hand in marriage. He made a long-term commitment to work seven years for his Uncle Laban so he could marry Rachel.

The Power of Love (Genesis 29:18-21)

This chapter in the Bible is the second time God records that a man loved his wife (the first was Isaac and Rebekah). Or, in Jacob's case, loved his wife-to-be. God states, "Now Jacob loved Rachel" (verse 18).

How much did Jacob love Rachel? The answer could be one of the most remarkable statements ever penned about the power of love: Jacob loved Rachel so much that he served seven years for Rachel, and "they seemed only a few days to him because of the love he had for her" (verse 20). And PS, a fast-forward view of their relationship reveals that Jacob's love for Rachel stood the test of time.

Seven years! That's how long Jacob's engagement lasted. And while he waited, his heart never swerved. His initial love-at-first-sight visual impression blossomed into a deep bond and full-out commitment. A crush, or puppy love, or lust is selfish and immature and in a hurry to get what it wants. Its slogan is, "I love you for what I can get from you—now." But true love says, "Your happiness is what I want most of all, and I'm willing to wait, if necessary, to be sure it's what's best for you." One of the greatest tests of true love is a willingness to wait.

The Deceiver Is Deceived (Genesis 29:21-30)

How does the saying go? "Your sin will find you out" (Numbers 32:23). There's also the saying, "What goes around, comes around." Well, that's what happened to Jacob.

Jacob was no stranger to deception. He had royally deceived his brother Esau, stealing Esau's birthright. And now the tables are turned on Jacob: His uncle is the one doing the deceiving, and Jacob is the victim. After all those years—seven of them!—Laban pulled the ultimate deception and switched his daughters when it came time for the wedding...and Jacob woke up married to a different woman!

How could this happen? Well, evidently Laban had persuaded the "different woman" to go along with the deception. That would be Leah, the older sister. Genesis 29:17 tells us "Leah's eyes were delicate," pointing to a physical flaw she had. She was covered with a veil. And Laban probably made sure Jacob had lots of wine to drink! And finally, the newlyweds were ushered into a dark tent—and voila! Laban married off his spinster elder daughter to Jacob.

We're not at all surprised to learn that Jacob did not love Leah, even though she was now his wife. Twice the Bible says that Leah was "unloved" (verses 31 and 33). And Jacob didn't give up on his mission to marry Rachel. He wasn't deterred by Laban's deception. When Jacob confronted Laban for what he had done, Laban offered to give Rachel to Jacob—for yet *another* seven years of servitude.

What did this mean for Jacob? It means that in a matter of only one week, he had acquired two wives—*and* had agreed to seven more years of hard labor.

No way this turns out well! We cringe as one of God's favored sons—one of the patriarchs of the Bible—enters into a bigamous relationship. This was absolutely not God's perfect will—then, now, or ever. As we saw with Adam and Eve, God designed one man for one woman (Genesis 2:24).

Be Careful What You Wish For (Genesis 29:31–30:34)

This crowded relationship that should never have existed—one man married to two sisters—went from bad to worse: Leah had several children, and Rachel was barren. In time, amid this stressful mess, Rachel's true character began to surface. She became intensely jealous of her sister, and quite possibly became the first-ever "drama queen." Can't you just imagine Rachel, standing with her head thrown back and her hands over her eyes, screaming, "Give me children, or else I die!" (30:1)? Not only was she blaming Jacob for the fact she had no children, but she was also essentially saying, "I'd rather be dead than live with this stigma of barrenness."

Here was a woman who had almost everything she could desire—beauty, wealth, a loving husband—and yet it wasn't enough. Rachel became envious, selfish, cranky, whiney, discontented, and demanding. Although she eventually gave birth to two sons, the sin of discontentment had already soured her relationship with her husband—and her sister.

In her marriage to Jacob, Rachel serves as an illustration of a discontented wife. And sad to say, many of today's husbands and wives are just as discontent. They blame each other and even God when there are no children, or when something else goes wrong. They're eaten up with frustration and they are eager to pin the blame elsewhere.

And once there are children, or once a problem has been resolved, these couples are still discontent! Now they can't wait until the kids leave the nest so they can move on with life. Or rather than remember other ways God has cared for their needs, they become preoccupied with the next thing they want or don't have. They're dissatisfied with their job, their pay, their home, their workplace.

What is the solution? The Bible says we are to narrow our focus: "Godliness with contentment is great gain. For we brought nothing into this world, and it is certain we can carry nothing out. And having food and clothing, with these we shall be content" (1 Timothy 6:6-8). The Bible tells us that contentment is something we must work at and learn. As the apostle Paul wrote, "I have *learned* in whatever state I am, to be content" (Philippians 4:11).

As a husband and wife team, be on the lookout for the poison of discontentment in your marriage. If you spot it, acknowledge it. Admit it. Discuss it. Then go to work together to deal with it. Draw on God's help to overcome this marriage crippler. Imagine the joy that will fill your home and marriage when you are singing God's praises for His daily goodness and provision for you!

A Family Without a Spiritual Leader (Genesis 31–35)

Now, we are talking about Jacob, right? Jacob of Abraham, Isaac, and Jacob—the patriarchs of the Bible? Why would we even infer that Jacob was not a spiritual leader for his family? After all, wasn't he God's handpicked man? Didn't God Himself speak to Jacob on his way to Haran? And also on the way back to his homeland? And again after he arrived in the land of Canaan?[7]

Yes, Jacob was God's man. He talked to God, was touched by God, and was taught by God. But, for some reason, his relationship with God failed to influence his wives and children. Jacob had a personal and powerful history with God, but that history was not successfully passed on to his family. Note just a few startling instances that point to Jacob's lack of spiritual influence on his family. (And here's a heads-up warning—it's pretty awful.)

- Jacob also fathered children by the two handmaids of Rachel and Leah—Bilhah and Zilpah (30:4,9).

- Jacob's wife Rachel took her father's household idols with her as Jacob was preparing to return home to Canaan (31:19).

- Two of Jacob's sons killed the men of Shechem, and the rest of his sons looted the city of Shechem because Jacob had failed to confront the men who had assaulted his daughter, Dinah (34).

- Out of envy, Jacob's sons connived to kill their brother, Joseph, but finally agreed to sell him into slavery instead (37:12-36).

- Reuben, Jacob's firstborn, slept with his father's concubine Bilhah (35:22).

After Jacob's family had been settled in the land of his birth (Canaan) for eight years, he finally commanded that they put away their foreign gods (Genesis 35:2). But it was too late. His children were grown-ups who had taken on some of their different mothers' (did we mention there were four?) religious practices.

Jacob could go right ahead and take away all the idols and religious jewelry, but history proved that his descendants still had problems with idolatry.

In the end, Jacob's spiritual concern for his family was too little, too late. The damage was done, and it had lasting consequences. In fact, the 12 tribes of Israel (one tribe for each of Jacob's 12 sons) were plagued with idolatry for another 1000 years. Unfortunately, in the life and household of Jacob, we see the devastating results of a lack of strong spiritual leadership on the part of the patriarch and head of the family.

Putting It All Together

The union of two people in marriage is potentially fraught with challenges—an understatement in the case of Jacob and Rachel! Their joining together was thwarted by a lying, conniving father-in-law, two wives, two concubines, and 12 sons generally marked by jealousy and aggressive, warlike behavior. No soap opera could ever even come close to duplicating all the angst, emotions, heartaches, and drama this clan lived with on a daily basis.

Even in a marriage absent of such problems, two individuals who think they know each other before the wedding suddenly find themselves living with a different person—a stranger. After the marriage vows are exchanged and the lovey-dovey thrill of the ceremony and honeymoon are over, everyday life seems to have a way of unearthing the real person behind those starry eyes.

Unlike you, Jacob woke up every day to two wives and two concubines. And, unlike you, after marrying Leah through Laban's trickery, he finally married Rachel, the woman he wanted. God's design is one woman plus one man in a marriage. Surely Jacob could have learned to love Leah—in the same way his father, Isaac, had loved his unseen, unknown bride, Rebekah. And here's the real rub: Over the long haul, Leah ended up being a better wife to Jacob than Rachel.

According to God's Word, you are to unconditionally love your partner in marriage and work at being God's kind of husband or wife. Once you are married, the real work of maintaining the relationship begins. Think of your marriage as a gift-wrapped present from the Lord. Its true value and appreciation comes after the gift is opened and you take time to enjoy it.

• Lessons for Wives from Rachel •

1. *When you must wait, be useful.* Rachel was a lady-in-waiting. She was just a young woman—probably a teenager—helping in the family business as a shepherdess. Her life and future was on hold as she waited to marry. How would God work in her life? The same way He works today: He used people, events, and circumstances.

On one particular day, God used all three types of catalysts—people, events, and circumstances—to set the direction for young Rachel's life. The event was the arrival of her cousin Jacob from a far country. The circumstance was the time of day for drawing water from the local well for the sheep. As for the people, God used Rachel and Jacob's family ties to bring the two together and introduce the possibility of marriage.

When your life is on hold, when you are in a waiting pattern, set goals. Stay busy. Be faithful. Pick a project. Be useful to others. I (Elizabeth) know so many missionary and military wives who have learned to stay busy bettering their lives and helping others. The same is true of my friends whose husbands travel extensively for their jobs.

Take a quick inventory of the pattern of your days, the people, events, and circumstances unique to your life. Even if these elements are not ideal, you can thank God that He has promised to work "all things" for your good, which includes the problem people, traumatic events, and difficult circumstances (Romans 8:28). God is always at work—sometimes in the open as with Rachel, and sometimes in the shadows.

2. *Your inner beauty matters most.* Rachel's beauty was skin-deep. She was described as being beautiful of form and appearance, but that's about as far as her beauty went. She was a whiner, a blamer, a deceiver, and a liar. She had everything, yet she was "envious, selfish, peevish, fretful, discontented, and demanding." [8]

By contrast, Rachel's sister, Leah, was not beautiful. She had weak eyes (Genesis 29:17), some form of physical defect. And yet, in spite of being flawed and unloved, she was a better wife to Jacob than the breathtakingly beautiful Rachel.

The Bible has much to say about the hidden person of the heart—"the incorruptible beauty of a gentle and quiet spirit, which is very precious in the sight of God" (1 Peter 3:4). External beauty soon fades away, but if you develop inner beauty by drawing close to the Lord and following Him with all your heart, your life will honor Him. You will be praised not only by God, but by your husband and children as well. "Charm is deceitful and beauty is passing, but a woman who fears the LORD, she shall be praised" (Proverbs 31:30).

3. *Fuel your faith daily.* Rachel had a weak view of God, and it tainted every part of her life. She grew up in a pagan culture, and her home contained pagan idols. For the first seven years of her marriage to Jacob, Rachel blamed everyone—including her husband—for her inability to have children. To Jacob she sobbed, "Give me children, or else I die!" (Genesis 30:1). She even resorted to the superstition of using a plant—mandrakes—as a possible remedy to become pregnant. This too failed.

It was only after she gave birth to her son Joseph that she rightly ascribed her motherhood to the Lord—"God has taken away my reproach" (30:23). However, when her family ran away from her father, Laban, she secretly stole the family idols (31:19). Why did she do this? Was it because she was leaving familiar surroundings and she wanted to take some "reminders" of home with her? Was it because she wanted to cover all her spiritual bases? Or did she buy into the general pagan consensus that these idols would help her with regard to fertility?

A solid faith seemed out of Rachel's grasp. It wasn't like God had failed to bless and provide—after all, her husband Jacob was very successful, and by now, she had even given birth to a son. Why, we wonder, would Rachel want to revert to her old religion?

And you? How closely can you identify with Rachel and her halfhearted faith? How strong—or weak—is your view of God? Are you acting and living like you believe in Him and trust in Him fully, or are you believing in yourself and relying on your own abilities? What you believe about God determines how you behave.

Take a look at your life and the evidence of your faith. Ask God to search your heart. Then pay attention to what He reveals. Fuel your faith daily by learning firsthand from God's Word about His power, His promises, and His provision. You'll be a stronger helpmate and mom—a real Rock of Gibraltar—for your family to lean on and count on.

4. *Have an attitude of gratitude.* Rachel was blessed with a hardworking husband who loved her and provided for her. And yet she was discontent. Why? Because she fixated on the one thing she didn't have—a child. And here's the kicker—in the same breath she used to name her newborn son, Joseph, she said she wanted more children! She uttered, "The LORD shall add to me another son" (Genesis 30:24).

Couples can get perplexed or angry with God when their dreams don't seem to be coming true. And even when the dreams do become reality, for some, it's never enough. It's no secret some couples are disgruntled and dissatisfied with their present homes, with their current jobs, with the amount of money they have or don't have—and on and on their murmurings go.

The sin of discontentment has infected countless marriages.

Today's society fosters a spirit of dissatisfaction. So make every effort to stop paying attention to the world and its selfish impulses. Turn things around by breaking the habit of negativity and complaining. You have thousands of promises from God to hold on to—including eternal life. If you recognize that the disease of discontentment is present in your marriage, quickly seek God's forgiveness and His help to overcome it. Ask God to open your eyes so you can identify His present blessings. They are many—too numerous to count! Then give thanks. Develop a habit of praising God. These new and positive responses will propel you toward an attitude of gratitude.

• Lessons for Husbands from Jacob •

1. *Let your wife in on the real you.* Jacob was not afraid to show his emotions. In an age when men didn't tend to show emotions, Jacob was extremely expressive. After his 400-mile journey, he was so happy to meet a relative that he immediately kissed Rachel and wept out loud. And he loved Rachel just as his father, Isaac, loved Rebekah. Jacob also openly, demonstratively mourned when he thought his son Joseph was dead. He tore his clothes, put on sackcloth and ashes, and mourned for Joseph many days, refusing to be comforted (Genesis 37:34-35).

Yes, Jacob was an emotional man, and you can definitely learn from his example of freely expressing his emotions. God has given you feelings, so let your wife in on them. One of the biggest complaints wives have about their husbands is their lack of openness. They don't know or aren't sure exactly what their husbands are thinking, feeling, or needing.

This brings us back to the importance of communication in marriage. Let your wife in on the real you. God intended the two of you to be one, but until you allow your wife to get inside you—to really know you, the real you—you are withholding something that would make you and your wife better and closer friends—best friends.

2. *"Practice looking out for the interests of others."* This is a practical translation of Philippians 2:4. [9]

Jacob was selfish. It's hard to gloss over this fact—he was a selfish brat. He wanted Esau's birthright and took it (never mind all the lying and trickery and greed that went along with getting it). He wanted his father's blessing, and allowed a willful mother to help him deceive his father. He wanted Rachel, and didn't care who he hurt in getting her. He wanted wealth, and seemed to show little interest in his family in the process.

Do we need to go on? The tragedy is that Jacob got everything he went after—but he lost his family in the process. God calls His people—and those of us who are husbands—to practice looking out for the interests of others, to be givers, to do good, to love sacrificially, to work diligently and provide for family. And Jesus calls us to go the extra mile. As husbands, let's not follow in Jacob's selfishness. Instead, let's turn our tendencies away from selfishness and toward sacrifice—sacrifice for our wives and our children. The results will be rewarding, and God will bless you and your family.

3. *Know who's Number One.* Jacob's love was divided. Tragically, bigamy was a common practice in Old Testament times. But it presented major relationship problems. It is impossible to love two people with the same intensity—or, in Jacob's case, four people (his two wives plus his two concubines, all mothers of his children).

When it comes to you and your wife, it's key that you know—and live out—your priorities. It's easy for a man to get distracted with his career, hobbies, and sports, and allow his love for his wife to take a backseat. As husbands, we are called to show a deep, sacrificial love that is willing to give all—even life itself—for the one loved. Nothing should stand between you and loving your spouse.

Not your career, your job, a hobby, a ministry, even your children. She's Number One on your Love List. Husbands, let's make these resolutions together:

- I resolve to tell my wife "I love you" every day.
- I resolve to show my love by my actions.
- I resolve to nurture my love for my wife.

4. *Be the spiritual leader you were meant to be.* You can't miss the fact that Jacob's faith in God was not passed on to his family. What stories he had to tell them about his personal encounters with God! Yet he failed to instruct his family in the ways of God. Living in a pagan land and in the midst of unbelieving family members isn't any different from what you face in your own family, neighborhood, and workplace.

The responsibility to provide spiritual leadership falls first on the shoulders of the man of the family—the husband, the dad. What are you doing to educate your family and ensure that the fundamentals of the faith are passed on to them? It's easy to get so busy doing your own thing that you neglect to provide strong spiritual direction for your family.

You don't have to be a seminary student or Bible study leader to provide such leadership. Start with your wife. Make sure the two of you share from God's Word together. How? Choose a devotional to work through. Watch a DVD or listen to Bible teaching on marriage and talk about what you learn. Attend a Sunday school class or Bible study. Whatever you decide to do, put forth the effort necessary to make it happen.

Then make sure you do the same with your kids. Deuteronomy 6:7 says parents are to faithfully talk to their kids about God and His Word throughout the day, during daily routines. Be sure your wife and children see and know that God is an important part of your life—the most important part. If you haven't started leading your family toward Christ, it's never too late. Start today!

5. *Remember, united you stand, divided you fall.* Jacob was hopelessly entangled with his in-laws—specifically his father-in-law, Laban. He was married to two of Laban's daughters. He was contracted to work for Laban for seven more years so he could marry Rachel. And he was financially tied to Laban. By the time Jacob broke his ties with Laban, Jacob had worked for him for 20 years. And, worst of all, during those 20 years, Jacob's family was immersed in Laban's pagan culture and beliefs.

Studies uniformly show that, of all the problems faced in a marriage, whether newlyweds or couples with decades under their belt, in-law problems rank first or second. The Number One reason for in-law issues is usually the failure on one spouse's part to "leave and cleave." In Genesis 2:24, God instructs husbands and wives with these words: "Therefore a man shall leave his father and mother and be joined to his wife, and they shall become one flesh."

If you have in-law issues, sit down with your wife and calmly talk about them. Communicate with each other about in-laws—and this includes brothers- and sisters-in-law. Pray and begin to make some joint decisions about what can or must be done, and what changes you can or must make. The purpose is to listen to each other and then set some guidelines or parameters together so you are both in agreement. Your goal? Be sure your extended family doesn't come between you and your spouse. The two of you are meant to be one flesh. And, as Jesus said, "What...God has joined together, let not man separate" (Matthew 19:6).

Building a Marriage that Lasts

Are you wondering what you can learn from Jacob and Rachel's relationship? Unfortunately, the takeaway truths are largely from the negative column. So let's focus on some fundamentals.

First, a solid foundation is mandatory. To last, a marriage and family must be built on love—love for God, and love for one another.

Jacob's family went off track because they didn't follow God's blueprint—at all! God's plan is for you to be fully committed to only one person—your mate. Do you want your marriage to be strong? Then go by the blueprint and do the work it takes to be a couple after God's own heart. Be faithful to your spouse.

Then grab your marriage toolbox and, once again, pull out communication. If you can talk about your problems, you can solve them, even if you agree that the solution is to get some advice to help you move forward.

A marriage that centers on wholeheartedly following God, is 100 percent dedicated to your spouse, and includes talking through all issues that threaten your marital relationship will become a marriage that lasts.

5

Manoah and His Wife

His mouth is most sweet, yes,
he is altogether lovely.
This is my beloved, and this is my friend.
SONG OF SOLOMON 5:16

Manoah grumbled as he stood in line with all his neighbors waiting for the burly Philistine to sharpen his farming tools. Daily life had been like this since the Philistine conquest almost 20 years earlier. To ensure that the Israelites didn't manufacture and stockpile sharp weapons, they were not allowed any means for maintaining or sharpening their own work tools. They were totally subservient to this warlike people who were not satisfied with their profits from sea trade. The Philistines also wanted the produce and profits that came from the rich farming land of Israel.

As he peered at the line of people ahead of him, Manoah could tell he was in for a long day. As usual, his time of waiting took his thoughts to his best friend, who just happened to be his wife. Maybe it was the occupation of their land by the oppressive

Philistines, or maybe it was his wife's "condition," but something had kept him and his wife closely connected all these years. Theirs was a unique marriage, and Manoah was already anxious to get back to his wife, who was probably feeling just as lonely. The couple had no children, and Manoah's wife was seen as cursed by others in the community, and shunned socially. She was viewed as a misfit. Manoah was glad his love and companionship had helped fill the empty void in her heart created by her barrenness and her being a social outcast.

What's Going On?

Israel's Disobedience (Judges 13:1)

You would think the children of Israel would have learned their lesson: Obedience to God means God's blessings. Disobedience to God means God's judgment. For several hundred years Israel had gone through repeated cycles of sin, servitude, supplication, and salvation (see Judges 1–12). And it had happened once again, and the people were now in the servitude phase. Poor Manoah was just one of the thousands who endured oppression because of the nation's moral decline.

Angelic Appearance #1 (Judges 13:2-5)

Hold on to your seat! You are about to witness one of the rarest of events in Old Testament history—the appearance of the Angel of the Lord! And He is about to appear to a woman whose name is never mentioned, the woman we know as Mrs. Manoah. She must have been a special lady to receive this kind of divine attention, and not just once, but twice! Here's what the Angel of the Lord said to our heroine, Manoah's wife:

> *He stated the obvious*—"you are barren" (verse 3).
>
> *He stated a prophecy*—"you shall conceive and bear a son" (verse 3).

He stated a precaution—"be careful not to drink wine or similar drink, and not to eat anything unclean" (verse 4).

He stated a separation—"no razor shall come upon his head, for the child shall be a Nazirite to God from the womb" (verse 5).

He stated a destiny—"he shall begin to deliver Israel out of the hand of the Philistines" (verse 5).

Mr. and Mrs. Manoah were given the honor of being the parents of an exceptional son whom they would name Samson. He would serve God and Israel as a judge for 20 years. His dramatic exploits would truly begin to deliver God's people and land from their archenemies, the Philistines.

Trusted Friend and Wife (Judges 13:6-8)

The Angel of the Lord gave Manoah's wife very specific and precise directions about the birth and raising of this unique child who was soon to be born. He also explained the boy's purpose. Immediately Mrs. Manoah went to her husband and repeated the Man of God's information and instructions about how they were to raise the child (verse 7).

Manoah's response? He never questioned his wife's story. He never once doubted her amazing tale. He fully believed and trusted what his wife communicated to him.

Then, as a concerned dad-to-be, Manoah went to God himself, not with doubt, but to ask for the wisdom he would need to raise this special child. He prayed, "O my Lord, please let the Man of God whom You sent come to us again and teach us what we shall do for the child who will be born" (verse 8).

Angelic Appearance #2 (Judges 13:9-12)

Manoah prayed for a return visit of the Angel of the Lord. And God answered his prayer. Once again, the Angel of the Lord appeared to Manoah's wife while she was alone in the field. This time she "ran in haste" to get Manoah and bring him to the field to see "the Man who came to me the other day [and] has just now appeared to me!" (verse 10).

Again, Manoah responded positively—without doubt or judgment—and listened to his wife. When he came to the Man, he said to Him, "Are you You the Man who spoke to this woman?" After the Angel of the Lord affirmed that He was, Manoah asked, "What will be the boy's rule of life, and his work?" (verse 12).

A Second Round of Instructions (Judges 13:13-14)

Manoah asked for guidance—and he got it. Speaking face-to-face with the Man of God, he was told that his wife held the keys to this boy's future. The Angel of the Lord said, "Of all that I said to the woman let her be careful. She may not eat anything that comes from the vine, nor may she drink wine or similar drink, nor eat anything unclean. All that I commanded her let her observe" (verses 13-14). These instructions were part of the Nazirite vow, which was taken by men or women who were set apart for God's service. In other words, the Angel of the Lord was declaring that Manoah's son was to be a Nazirite, set apart for God's use (see Numbers 6).

A Final Realization (Judges 13:15-24)

With a heart full of deep gratitude to God, Manoah wanted to extend Middle Eastern hospitality. So he offered to feed this messenger, not knowing He was the Angel of the Lord. The Angel of the Lord then instructed Manoah to offer the food to the Lord instead. As Manoah placed the food on the altar, the Angel of the Lord was taken up in the flame. At this point, Manoah completely lost it. The realization hit him—he was in the presence of God! He was absolutely certain that both of them would surely die, for they had seen God.

It takes a special lady to calm down a man after something this earth-shattering. And it takes a great measure of wisdom to reassure someone that, if God had wanted to kill him, it would have already happened. Mrs. Manoah was this lady. She quietly steadied her husband, who agreed that her logic made sense. And, as the saying goes, the rest is history. Judges 13 closes with the birth of Samson, the promised son who would grow up to lead the nation of Israel against the Philistines.

A Faithful Set of Parents (Judges 13:24–14:10)

We actually thought of calling this section "the care and feeding of a 'strong'-willed kid," but, after sharing a laugh, decided against it. But you get the picture, right? Parenting, if it is God's will for you, is probably the hardest work you will ever do!

Thankfully, Manoah and his wife were given explicit instructions by the angel on how to raise their unique son. The guidelines even included Manoah's wife, the mom-to-be. In short, she was to be careful not to drink wine or similar drink, nor eat anything unclean. "For behold, you shall conceive and bear a son. And no razor shall come upon his head, for the child shall be a Nazirite to God from the womb" (Judges 13:5).

From the Bible text it appears that Manoah and his wife did their best to raise this extraordinary boy—a boy whom the angel said would "begin to deliver Israel out of the hand of the Philistines" (verse 5). Because of his unusual beginnings, Samson's parents probably repeated the story of the miracle of the angel's appearance and the angelic being's instructions to Samson often. What little boy wouldn't want to hear this story over and over…and over? So, as Samson began to physically mature, he most likely retained much of what he had been taught. He was probably proud of his long hair, a result of keeping the law of the Nazirite. And he realized God had a special calling on his life.

However, as Samson grew older, some major character flaws began to show up:

He was willful—he went against his parents' wishes and married a Philistine girl (14:1-3).

He was vengeful—he used his great God-given strength for his own purposes rather than God's purposes (15:7).

He was lustful—he had relations with a harlot (16:1).

Fortunately, for parents like Manoah and his wife—for those who have a strong-willed and wayward child—it's never too late to pray for that child to receive a spiritual wake-up call and look to God in repentance. That's the silver lining in this cloud of rebellion and self-will. At the end of his heroic and colorful life, the last words spoken by Samson were addressed to God. Samson uttered a prayer to God and a plea of repentance and trust as he sacrificed himself in his role as judge and protector of God's people, killing several thousand prominent Philistines and their leaders. He called to the Lord, saying, "O Lord GOD, remember me, I pray! Strengthen me, I pray, just this once, O God, that I may with one blow take vengeance on the Philistines" (16:28).

How did God respond?

> And Samson took hold of the two middle pillars which supported the temple [where the Philistines were worshipping their false gods], and he braced himself against them, one on his right and the other on his left. Then Samson said, "Let me die with the Philistines!" And he pushed with all his might, and the temple fell on the lords and all the people who were in it (verses 29-30).

These final words point to Samson's efforts in his service to God: "So the dead that he killed at his death were more than he had killed in his life" (verse 30).

Putting It All Together

From what we see in Scripture, Manoah and his wife had an outstanding relationship. They were blessed to be best friends. And they really needed each other! They lived in a time of spiritual and moral darkness. Godly examples were in short supply. Yet they did their best as a couple to please God and follow His instructions. This man and woman present husbands and wives with a checklist of what it means to be a couple after God's own heart—a checklist they passed with flying colors! And it's a checklist you should strive to emulate. Here goes:

They were simple people who did not have privileges, rank, or wealth. They were content with the little they had, with the life they lived, and with each other. They readily shared all of the little and large events of daily life with each other. They had no problem communicating with one another. They listened carefully, believed what was said, and took advice from each other. They trusted and didn't question each other. They shared a strong faith in God and His promise to them. They were willing to work together to raise their future child in the way God specified.

In other words, they were best friends.

• Lessons for Wives from Manoah's Wife •

1. *Trusting God is a daily choice.* It is possible to live victoriously with pain and painful circumstances. The precious wife in this chapter—Mrs. Manoah—was not sick with a physical affliction or a disease, nor did she have mental problems. No, her pain came from being childless. As if her own heart's aching and sorrow wasn't enough, her society treated barren women as outcasts. These unfortunate women were treated almost like lepers! They were even suspected of being punished by God for some secret sin.

How does a woman with an affliction, a lack, a loss, a painful sorrow live with her suffering? Many women denounce their faith in God and turn their backs on Him. Or they become hardened and bitter. But how much better to take a page out of Mrs. Manoah's book! She let her pain press her closer to God. God was always a valued and comforting part of her life. Trusting God was and is—and always will be—the right choice to make in managing your trials.

What is your situation? Your sorrow of heart? What daily challenge are you experiencing? Is it the anguish of a rocky marriage? The pain of a disobedient child—or the lack of a child? Whatever it is, do as Manoah's wife did. Lift your pain up to God and let Him use it to empower your faith. Take to heart these triumphant words from Christ Himself, spoken to the apostle Paul in the midst of Paul's suffering and pain: "My grace is sufficient for you, for My strength is made perfect in weakness" (2 Corinthians 12:9).

2. *Be the helper you were meant to be.* Provide balance in your marriage. There's no doubt that Manoah was a strong leader. Just look at the way he got involved, got the facts, and handled the visit from the Angel of the Lord. But in his moment of fear or panic, when it dawned on him that he and his wife had been in God's presence and therefore would surely die, his wife came to the rescue and provided wisdom and a practical perspective.

He said, "We shall surely die, because we have seen God!" (Judges 13:22).

She said, "If the LORD had desired to kill us, He would not have accepted a burnt offering and a grain offering from our hands, nor would He have shown us all these things, nor would He have told us such things as these at this time" (verse 23).

Both were right. In Exodus 33:20, God told Moses, "No man shall see Me, and live." But, as Manoah's wife observed, the two of them were still alive and well.

We've seen over and over again that, as a wife, you are your husband's helper. You are meant to be his complement—to complete him, to balance him. You are his partner in life. The two of you are a team. Hopefully when your husband is down or discouraged, you can come alongside him with a word of encouragement. And vice versa. Every step you take to grow in the Lord makes you a stronger partner.

3. *Remember your priorities.* Manoah's wife lived out God's priorities. There may have been other women working with her in the field that day when the Angel of the Lord first appeared to her, or a few girlfriends she could have confided in, but she bypassed all these secondary people and made a beeline straight to her husband. He was the person she wanted to tell first. He was the priority person in her life. He was her best friend, her partner in life and marriage. She honored her husband by going directly to him with this important news.

Uh-oh. Who do you turn to first with good news? Is your husband always the first to know anything that's important to you? Do you keep information to yourself until your husband knows? In God's list of priorities—and priority people in your life—as a married woman, your husband is Number One. He tops the list ahead of your parents, sisters, and friends…and definitely your Facebook friends! If your husband is your best friend, he will always be the first person you'll want to share news with—any news.

4. *Aim for faith for the big—and little—things in life.* Manoah's wife possessed great faith. This woman was surprised and showered with the most wonderful news from the Most Wonderful Person in all of creation—the Lord! How did she react in the presence of God? With great calm and dignity. Simply put, she handled it by and with faith. She didn't question God or His message. She didn't interrogate Him about His means or methods. She requested no signs and showed no hint of doubt. She responded with the rare and precious silence of belief.

How do you respond to the promises of God? Do you trust them and take them at face value? Is your faith marked by silent acceptance—no questions asked? By a gentle spirit—no details needed? By a sweet submissiveness—no struggle offered?

• Lessons for Husbands from Manoah •

1. *Live and lead with confidence.* Manoah could have been pretty nasty and shown contempt when his wife—and not him—was visited by the "Man of God." God obviously saw Manoah's wife as a worthy partner and complement to his own spiritual maturity. And besides that, she had very good news to bring home.

Like Manoah, you should not be threatened by your wife's spiritual growth. She is not in competition with your leadership. Her maturity should bolster your role as a leader! The Proverbs 31 woman was a marvelous wife whose accomplishments were known far and wide. Within the context of her many exploits, God says, "Her husband is known in the gates, when he sits among the elders of the land" (verse 23).

As a husband, make sure you encourage your wife in her study of God's Word. If there's a women's Bible study in the evening, take your turn putting the kids to bed or helping around the house so she can attend. Her spiritual growth will benefit not only her but you and the kids. Your wife's spiritual maturity should be top priority for you.

2. *Make a rule to pray about everything.* Manoah had a relationship with God. As soon as he was told of the visit from the Angel of the Lord, Manoah immediately went to God in prayer. The closer you are to God, the more immediately you'll include God in the events and details of your life. Here's a way to test your spiritual maturity—the next time you have an issue to resolve or a decision to make, ask yourself: *How quickly will I seek God's help through prayer?*

3. *Manoah was a man of faith.* Scripture says faith "is the substance of things hoped for, the evidence of things not seen" (Hebrews 11:1). This verse certainly describes Manoah's faith. Surely he had been hoping for a child. His culture and his profession as a farmer demanded children. His faith rose to the surface when his wife said an angel had told her they were going to have a child. He didn't question the news or hesitate even for a second in believing it would be so. What an amazing show of faith!

Who was Manoah anyway? He was a simple farmer. And how did the news come to him? Secondhand, from his wife. As amazing as the news was, and considering he didn't hear it himself, he still believed. He instantly showed unquestioning faith. You and I, like Manoah, don't need a pedigree or a postgraduate degree to exhibit faith. And we don't need a burning bush or a ladder coming down out of heaven. We just need to believe God's Word. Faith is just believing what God says He will do.

4. *Leading requires getting the facts straight.* Manoah was the leader in his marriage, and he was also a learner. How does a guy learn? He asks questions. He seeks answers. He's never satisfied with the status quo. Manoah was definitely that kind of guy. He asked about the child. He asked about the angel. He asked for instruction on how to raise his future child. He wanted to learn as much as he could about what was going on in his family.

Here was a simple farmer providing us with a shining example of a desire to learn. If you are to lead in your marriage and family, at work, and at church, you must be a learner.

Building a Marriage that Lasts

What a great couple to model your marriage after! And it's obvious what the foundation of Manoah and his wife's marriage was: They were best friends—best friends forever! What does it take to be best friends? Mutual, undying love for each other. Spending time together. Talking things over. Trusting each other. And praying for one another.

God's blueprint for a great marriage is right here in front of us: Both as partners and individuals, this husband-wife team lived out their roles and responsibilities as set down by God. Manoah's wife sought out her husband as soon as she heard from the Angel of the Lord, and Manoah took the leadership reins and prayed, talked with the Angel of the Lord, and secured all the facts and details they would need as a couple to raise a boy who became "Earth's Strongest Man." [10]

And we cannot miss the tools Manoah and his wife used to live as a couple after God's own heart, a couple who were best friends. Prayer? Check. Communication? Check. Mutual trust? Check. And an unwavering faith in God? Check.

God's love through the Holy Spirit is available to you as a couple for building your own foundation of friendship for a marriage after God's own heart. And God's blueprint for your roles as husband and wife never changes. It will guide and direct you all the days of your marriage. And His tools? They are available—if you choose to put them to work in your home and your marriage.

Signs You and Your Spouse Are Not Best Friends

You are unable to talk about any and everything.

You tell someone else things you haven't or wouldn't tell your spouse.

You are more comfortable in a group than you are together.

When you think of your "best friend" your spouse isn't the person you name.

When you and your spouse are together, you have nothing meaningful to say.

You are not in any hurry to get home to see your spouse after work. In fact, you often think of excuses to stay away from home.

6

Boaz and Ruth

A Couple with Character

So she fell on her face, bowed down to the ground,
and said to him, "Why have I
found favor in your eyes,
that you should take notice of me,
since I am a foreigner?"

RUTH 2:10

Imagine the darkest, blackest night you have ever experienced. Maybe you were camping in a wilderness, or out on a boat away from city lights, or perhaps your town was hit by a power outage. It was so dark and so black you couldn't see anything…except the stars in God's heaven, which appeared even brighter than usual due to the black void of space.

The "stars" of the book of Ruth are Boaz and Ruth. And are they ever shining! The story of their beautiful romance occurs against the dark background of godlessness in Israel. It takes place during the time of the judges, a time when "there was no king in Israel; everyone did what was right in his own eyes" (Judges 17:6).

Into the hopelessness of a terribly dark time in the history of God's people, Boaz and Ruth make their appearance, lighting up the pages of Scripture. Their hearts blaze so brilliantly that they spark a glimmer of hope for the future in the hearts of the people. Boaz was a single man of godly character, and Ruth was a widow of godly character. Read on to see the spectacular way in which God brought these two faithful followers of Him together...and how their love and marriage can still make a difference in your life today.

A Look at the Backstory

It has now been 1000 years since God called Abraham out of Ur. At that time, God promised to make Abraham a great nation. When Jacob, Abraham's grandson, took his family to Egypt to protect them from a severe famine in the land of Canaan, there were only 70 people in their group (Genesis 46:27). But after 400 years, with much of that time spent in slavery, God's people had become a force estimated at two million.

This teeming multitude ultimately conquered the land God had promised to them. But it wasn't long before sin and disobedience plunged the people and the land into chaos. But God is faithful. During this dark and turbulent period, He graced the world with a truly amazing love story. In this refreshing account of a couple after God's own heart we see a delightful and charming picture of domestic life in a time of anarchy and trouble. It is a love story of opposites coming together:

> One was poor, and the other rich.
> One was a Moabite, and the other a Jew.
> One worshipped idols, and the other worshipped God.
> One possessed nothing, the other offered everything.

Yet with their many opposites, this couple had one thing in common—their strength of character. But unlike other love stories that have a happy ending, theirs is a story that has no ending. Why? Because Boaz and Ruth were the start of a family—a genealogy—that, in another 1000 years, would bring forth the Messiah, the Savior of the world, Jesus Christ the Lord. He, the Christ, would sit on the throne of King David, who just happened to be the great-grandson of Boaz and Ruth. And His kingdom would have no end.

What's Going On?

The Famine and Funerals (Ruth 1:1-5)

Meet Elimelech, an Israelite who, along with his wife, Naomi, and their two sons, left their home in Bethlehem to escape a famine. They moved to Moab, a country southeast of Bethlehem. When Elimelech died and left Naomi a widow, their two sons married Moabite women. Then, ten years later, the sons also died, leaving their two wives as widows.

The Farewells and the Faith of Ruth (Ruth 1:6-18)

Hearing now that there was abundant food in Bethlehem, Naomi decided to return to her homeland. As she set out on her journey, both of her daughters-in-law determined to join her. But as they packed up to leave, a bitter and broken Naomi urged her daughters-in-law, Orpah and Ruth, to stay in Moab and begin the next phase of their lives among their own people.

Orpah decided to remain with her family. But not Ruth. She vowed to accompany her mother-in-law and embrace Naomi's God as her God too. One of the greatest declarations of devotion in the Bible was uttered by Ruth to Naomi:

> Entreat me not to leave you, or to turn back from following after you; for wherever you go, I will go; and wherever you lodge, I will lodge; your people shall be my people, and your God, my God. Where you die,

I will die, and there will I be buried. The LORD do
so to me, and more also, if anything but death parts
you and me (1:16-17).

The Encounter with Boaz (Ruth 2:1-7)

The two widows, Naomi and Ruth, made the journey back to
Bethlehem. They arrived tired and destitute after weeks of travel.
Where could they find food? The Law of Moses commanded that
the corners of every field should not be harvested so the poor
could come behind the harvesters and gather up the leftovers. Ruth
gallantly volunteered to glean the leftover grain from the fields of
Naomi's relative, Boaz, so she and Naomi could have food to eat.

Bethlehem was a small village in which everyone knew each
other, so when Boaz arrived at the field to offer a blessing to his
workers, it didn't take long for him to notice there was a stranger
among them, Ruth. He inquired about her, and "the servant who
was in charge of the reapers answered and said, 'It is the young
Moabite woman who came back with Naomi from the country
of Moab'" (verse 6).

The Encouragement to Ruth (Ruth 2:8-17)

Right away Boaz told Ruth to stay in his field. He had already
heard of her devotion to Naomi and praised her for her kindness to her mother-in-law. To show his appreciation, Boaz invited
Ruth to eat from the meal he provided for his harvesters. Boaz
then instructed the workers to leave ample heads of barley in the
field for Ruth!

The Praise of Naomi (Ruth 2:18-23)

When Ruth returned home with a surprisingly large bundle of
grain, she told Naomi about Boaz's kindness. Naomi then blessed
Boaz and told Ruth that he was a close relative who, according to
Jewish law, could marry her and "redeem" the property of Naomi's

dead husband, Elimelech. The provision of a "kinsman-redeemer" is a major theme of the book of Ruth.

The Plan (Ruth 3:1-5)

Wanting to provide a home for Ruth, Naomi gave Ruth instructions for presenting herself as a potential wife for Boaz. She then sent Ruth to find Boaz at the threshing floor. Ruth was told to wait until Boaz finished his meal, and then lie down at his feet.

The Proposal and the Problem (Ruth 3:6-13)

In the middle of the night a startled Boaz awakened to find Ruth lying at his feet. She then, as instructed, asked him to perform his duties as her family redeemer. As much as he wanted to do exactly as Ruth proposed, Boaz knew there was another man more closely related to her and Naomi than he was. According to the Law, that man must first be offered the opportunity to wed Ruth. As Boaz explained to Ruth, if that relative would not marry her, then he most gladly would.

The Precaution and the Provision (Ruth 3:14-18)

Boaz next requested that Ruth stay at the threshing floor until dawn, and then secretly leave so her visit would not be interpreted negatively by anyone who saw her there. Then, to prove his commitment to follow through on her request, Boaz sent Ruth home with six measures of barley. Naomi had probably waited up all night, pacing the floor, until Ruth returned home. As Ruth related what Boaz had said, Naomi noticed she had a large amount of grain. Naomi then reassured Ruth that Boaz "will not rest until he has concluded the matter this day" (verse 18).

The Decision Is Made (Ruth 4:1-12)

At the town gate, Boaz, true to his word, met with the other relative and ten town leaders as witnesses. Boaz reminded the other man that he had the right to the first chance to buy the dead Elimelech's land. The man was interested, but Boaz added that the buyer must also marry Ruth. The other kinsman then declined to buy the land, for doing so would endanger his own estate. The family redeemer offered Boaz the estate and validated the transaction in front of witnesses.

The Dynasty Begins (Ruth 4:13-22)

At last, Ruth became Boaz's wife, and later she gave birth to a son. Then the women in Bethlehem said to Naomi, "Blessed be the LORD, who has not left you this day without a close relative; and may his name be famous in Israel!" (verse 14). Little did Boaz and Ruth know that this birth would ultimately demonstrate God's goodness on a lost world—for in God's marvelous plan, Boaz and Ruth ended up becoming the great-grandparents of King David, in the lineage of Jesus Christ!

Putting It All Together

God is always faithful—to His people and to His plan. Two poverty-stricken widows arrived in Bethlehem with little more than the thin threads on their backs. They had no husbands, no family, no funds, no food. All they had was the willingness of the younger and stronger of the two women to labor in the fields, gleaning the leftover grain reserved for the poor.

But God was aware. God was guiding. He was leading. He was at work. He brought forth a godly man to redeem and care for this brave feminine team of in-laws who were a part of the bloodline from which the Savior of the world would come.

In this short book of the Bible, we are blessed by a real glimpse of God's loving care and oversight of His people. We are blessed by watching God work on His greater plan—a plan that would lead to Jesus. We are blessed to see a woman and her mother-in-law working as a loving, helpful, and respectful team. We are blessed to see up close the many worthy character qualities in the man Boaz. And we are blessed to witness the courtship and marriage of Boaz and Ruth, along with the arrival of their first baby, as God blessed His faithful people.

Now, for a few lessons in love.

• Lessons for Wives from Ruth •

1. *In-laws are family.* Ruth was faced with a choice. Her husband was dead, and her husband's mother, Naomi, also a widow, was heading back to her homeland. Naomi had given both her daughters-in-law an open door and her blessing to go back to their people, to their families. Ruth's sister-in-law chose to walk through that door and return to her family home. But Ruth chose to go with Naomi, and what's even more important, Ruth chose Naomi's God.

In spite of all the in-law jokes you hear almost daily, your in-laws are still your family and should be treated as such—with love and respect. Ruth chose to make Naomi her second mom, and followed Naomi's advice and counsel even when it meant sacrificing her pride. The two of them became quite a team as together they took on the life-and-death challenge of survival.

Hopefully you have a mom-in-law who's like Naomi—one you can confide in, lean on when you need advice, and trust. I know Jim's mom—my mother-in-law—was one of these special people. But if your in-laws are not as friendly or supportive or helpful as you would hope, please, don't give up on them! Make an effort to stay in touch through phone calls, cards, emails, and visits. And you'll definitely want them to see their exceptionally smart and good-looking grandkids!

Now, if you happen to be a mother-in-law yourself, look to

Naomi as your model. Be your daughter-in-law's Number One cheerleader, the president of her support group. Like Naomi, if you are there for your kids and their spouses, they will become treasured additions to your family.

2. *Having a mentor is a blessing.* Ruth was a foreigner. She didn't know the culture in Israel or what was expected of her by the locals in Bethlehem. But how fortunate she was to have Naomi as her mentor. Naomi rolled up her sleeves and rolled out the love and set about coaching Ruth through the rigors of gleaning in the fields, teaching her how to act around the owner of the fields and the workers, and most important of all, how to conduct herself when it came to marriage prospects.

Having a mentor means you are willing to submit to that person's guidance. Do you have all the answers to the Christian life, to making a marriage work, to raising your children? You know you don't. So humble yourself and follow the advice given in Titus 2:3-5. Make a point of getting to know an "older woman" who can show you from the Bible what you need to know to deal with the many issues you face as a wife.

3. *Develop faithfulness even in the little things.* Ruth came to Naomi's hometown ready to serve her mother-in-law. She was prepared to sacrifice everything to faithfully assist Naomi. She was even willing to go into the harvest fields day after day and faithfully pick up the tiny pieces of grain that had been left by the harvesters for those like her and Naomi, who were poor and needy. This little act of service to her mother-in-law was not only appreciated by Naomi, but also endeared Ruth to the people of Bethlehem, and especially Boaz.

Faithfulness is a fruit of the Spirit and is essential for you as a wife. And because your husband is counting on you, faithfulness must be part of your daily walk. Faithfulness means your husband can count on you to do what you say you will do, be where you say you will be, and do what needs to be done. How would you rate your faithfulness even in the little things...like the laundry?

4. *Godly character is a magnet.* Ruth arrived in Bethlehem as a stranger, but soon she gained the attention and respect of the whole town—including Boaz. Why? Because of all that she had done for her mother-in-law (Ruth 2:11). As Boaz stated, "All the people of my town know that you are a virtuous woman" (3:11). Her faithful service to her mother-in-law was noticed and was a reflection of Ruth's godly character, her inner beauty.

Your character is like a magnet in your home. Everyone, starting with your husband, will be affected and drawn to God's love and goodness through your influence. If you want to see changes in the spiritual tone of your home and marriage, start with your own life. Your consistent walk by God's Spirit betters the life of your husband.

5. *Accept the help of others.* Ruth and Naomi came to Bethlehem in a desperate condition, but they came as a team. Each woman needed help, and each woman gave help. Neither one said, "No thanks. I'm good. I've got this." No, God used each woman to help the other. God also used those who harvested the grain fields according to the law by leaving a certain amount of grain for the poor (like Naomi and Ruth) to pick up. God used Boaz to ensure that Naomi and Ruth, two destitute widows, had the food they needed—and extra! And ultimately, God used the faith, commitment, and generous heart of Boaz to fully meet the two widows' needs as Boaz married Ruth, guaranteeing provision for her future. When God wants to use others to take care of you, be gracious, be thankful, and humbly accept their help.

• Lessons for Husbands from Boaz •

Many modern love stories portray one member of the couple as being a little stronger, a little more loving, a little more giving, maybe even somewhat more noble of character than the other. Well, this is not the case with Ruth and Boaz. They are both equally worthy of a detailed study. And they both had many qualities that demand attention. You've seen a few of Ruth's many qualities in the section above for wives. Now it's time to look at Boaz. And there's a lot to look at!

1. *Diligent*—Boaz is described as "a man of great wealth" (Ruth 2:1), and we see him carefully and thoughtfully overseeing his property. We see here that he is a man of diligence.

Proverbs 10:4 tells us that laziness, or a "slack hand," leads to poverty. God expects His men to work and work hard to provide for their wives and families. We are told, "If anyone does not provide for his own, and especially for those of his household, he has denied the faith and is worse than an unbeliever" (1 Timothy 5:8). God even goes so far as to command, "If anyone will not work, neither shall he eat" (2 Thessalonians 3:10). You may never be a wealthy man, but as you are faithful and conscientious in your work, God will bless your diligence and provide for you and your family.

A diligent man will be successful not only at work, but also at home. A diligent husband pays attention to his wife and her needs and safety. And a diligent dad purposefully invests time in his relationships with his children, in their character development, and their training in taking care of their responsibilities. A diligent overseer takes care of his home, property, and finances. Take a look around. Is anything—or anyone—being neglected? If so, take note and take care of it. Be diligent.

2. *Merciful*—Noticing Ruth hard at work, Boaz asked his workers about her situation. Upon learning the facts, he then had mercy on her and her plight and acted on her behalf (Ruth 2:7).

Mercy is the ability for a man to show grace, sympathy, tolerance, and understanding toward others. Maybe this is what Peter meant when he wrote, "Husbands, likewise, dwell with them with understanding, giving honor to the wife, as to the weaker vessel, and as being heirs together of the grace of life." Then Peter added a warning to husbands: "that your prayers may not be hindered" (1 Peter 3:7).

Boaz showed mercy by being concerned about Ruth. He acted to find out what she needed. Then he supplied what was lacking. In his mercy, he wanted to come to her aid with whatever would help her most.

How can you be more merciful to your wife? Begin by being more observant of her needs. More aware of how you can give her a hand, or ease a burden, or take over one or two of her responsibilities. She will be blessed, and so will you when you cultivate this godlike quality. Jesus said, "Blessed are the merciful, for they shall obtain mercy" (Matthew 5:7).

3. *Godly*—The first words spoken by Boaz as he entered his field and blessed his workers tells the story of his love for God: "Now behold, Boaz came from Bethlehem, and said to the reapers, 'The LORD be with you!'" (Ruth 2:4). Later, after finding out who Ruth was, Boaz prayed and asked God to bless Ruth in return for her care for Naomi (verse 12).

Boaz showed sincere love and care for the welfare of his workers and, as the story of his relationship with Ruth unfolds, we see his godly character going into action as he comes to the rescue of this poor Moabite widow.

Are you and your spouse having problems? A good place to start damage control is with your relationship with God. Are you reading your Bible? Praying? Regularly taking care of any sin issues? If these areas are failing to get your attention, then this is the place to start strengthening your bond with your wife. A husband's relationship with his God will be mirrored in his relationship with his wife.

4. *Encouraging*—Boaz pointed out Ruth's strong qualities and spoke of them to cheer her on: "It has been fully reported to me, all that you have done for your mother-in-law since the death of your husband, and how you have left your father and your mother and the land of your birth, and have come to a people whom you did not know before" (2:11). Surely these words of encouragement were like raindrops on the parched desert sand of Ruth's heart.

Of all the people in the world who need to be encouraged, it is our wives. Their work is never done. Their roles and responsibilities never seem to end! As a husband, you are to be her Number One cheerleader. Open your eyes to all she does for you and others. Then count the ways you can openly and personally praise and encourage her.

5. *Faithful*—Naomi called it when she told Ruth, "Sit still, my daughter...for the man will not rest until he has concluded the matter this day" (3:18). Boaz followed through on the promise he had made to Ruth—that he would approach the other kinsman who had the first right to marry her. And he did. He went to the elders at the city gate to clear the way to marry Ruth (4:1).

Marriage is a contract in which two people vow fidelity to each other. A husband who is faithful in what he says and does can be trusted, and trust is the glue that holds a marriage together. A wife will follow her husband to the ends of the earth if she knows she can trust him and that he has her best interests at heart at all times.

Trust is fragile. It is slowly obtained over time as you persevere and build up a good track record, but can be lost in an instant. It takes only one lie, one indiscretion, one failure to follow through to topple a lifetime of trust.

Building a Marriage that Lasts

Each couple in this study has so much to teach about what it takes to build a marriage that lasts. As we say farewell to Boaz and Ruth, we are thankful for the solid foundation upon which they built their spectacular marriage—a heart for God. Each spouse was godly. Each lived to serve God wholeheartedly. Each trusted God—His Law, His Word, and His plan for their lives. When both you and your spouse actively focus on developing godly character qualities, the foundation of your marriage will be twice as strong.

God's Word is the divine blueprint that shows you how to build every part of your life, including marriage. Both Boaz and Ruth desired to do what was right based on God's Word, to do what pleased the Lord. Because of this deep overarching desire, God paved the way for them to find each other and fall in love.

In Boaz and Ruth you have front-row seats for observing diligence, devotion, patience, thoughtfulness, discretion, generosity, compassion, and honesty in a marriage. It's obvious these many godly character qualities combined to create a couple after God's own heart. Are any of these tools missing in your toolbox?

7

David and Bathsheba

Second-chance Marriage

The LORD also has put away your sin;
you shall not die.

2 SAMUEL 12:13

It was a warm spring evening in Jerusalem, and the king was strolling the roof of his palace. His most trusted general, Joab, was battling against the armies of Ammon, and David had chosen to do something unusual this time—he had stayed home rather than fight with his army.

David stretched and sighed as he rounded a corner of the palace rooftop. Yes, life was good, and it was nice to have some time to himself. Then he slammed to a stop and blinked, wondering if what he saw in front of him could possibly be real.

Yes, sure enough, as he looked down on the homes around the palace, he noticed on one rooftop a woman enjoying a bath. Sight...led to desire...which led to formulating a plan...which culminated in action: David sent several trusted men to the home of the woman with instructions to bring her to the king's palace.

What began as simple lust set in motion a complex string of events that would ultimately bring great grief and havoc upon David's own family, and many others around him. David's actions affirm what the prophet Hosea predicted in Hosea 8:7: "They sow the wind, and reap the whirlwind."

What's Going On?

Just about everyone has experienced a watershed moment that seems to change the course of their life. For Jim, as I've heard him often share, it was the Sunday morning at the University of Oklahoma when he decided not to go to church so he could study for a big exam on Monday. He had gone to church every Sunday since enrolling at the university, but this was only going to be a one-time emergency miss. Then guess what? The next Sunday it was easy to make the same decision to again miss church and hit the books. It wasn't long before Jim wasn't going to church at all… and that's when he met me—down in the pit!

In this chapter you are about to enter into David's watershed event. Up until chapter 11 of 2 Samuel, David has been presented as the ideal servant of the Lord—the man after God's own heart, who obeyed every point of the law and zealously implemented each command. As a result, God blessed David and the nation of Israel beyond anything that could have been imagined.

But things were about to change.

David Evaded His Responsibilities (2 Samuel 11:1)

Second Samuel 11 opens with this statement: "It happened in the spring of the year, at the time when kings go out to battle, that David sent Joab and his servants with him, and all Israel; and they destroyed the people of Ammon and besieged Rabbah. But David remained at Jerusalem" (verse 1). I'm sure you've been told by a well-meaning teacher or your parents that "an idle mind is the devil's playground." Because David hadn't gone to war, as is expected of a king, he had little to do—and he ended up in the wrong place at the wrong time. He was where he was not supposed to be. There in his residence, as he roamed the halls, corridors, and rooftop of the palace, he was primed for getting into trouble.

Too much free time can be a bad thing. Keeping your commitments; taking care of business; and focusing on your family, home, and job responsibilities is a good thing! Being where you are supposed to be and doing what you are supposed to be doing keeps you centered and accountable.

David Lingered in Temptation (2 Samuel 11:2-4)

Most people tend to confuse temptation with sin. David's temptation occurred when he spotted a woman taking a bath. His sin was lingering over the scene...lingering long enough to take in her beauty and long enough to set the wheels of sin in motion by inquiring about her, sending for her, and finally sleeping with her.

When temptation is not dealt with, it leads to sin. Chapter 1 of this book featured Adam and Eve. Do you remember Eve's sin? "When the woman saw that the tree was good for food, that it was pleasant to the eyes, and a tree desirable to make one wise, she took of its fruit and ate. She also gave to her husband with her, and he ate" (Genesis 3:6). Eve's sin followed the same progression as David's: She was tempted when she saw the tree with the desirable fruit, and her sin began when she wanted the fruit...which led to taking the fruit...which led to eating the fruit.

What's the solution? How can you handle temptation so it doesn't lead to sinful acts? God says you are not to linger over temptation. Instead you are to flee. Christians—both male and female, husbands and wives—are to "flee...youthful lusts" (2 Timothy 2:22).

A hotbed for temptation is the workplace, where "workplace romances" are a real fact of life. As a couple, whenever either one of you is around other people, and especially at work, where everyone puts their best foot forward, it's tempting to become attracted to one of your workmates. At work, everything is generally upbeat and problem-free, and everyone tells you what you want to hear. At work there is freedom from accountability and from the realities of home where real life comes loaded with marital strife, crying or rebellious kids, and a mile-long list of chores. Oh, and don't forget that mountain of bills.

At the first sign of any kind of flirting, or of someone paying too much attention to you, or of a growing attraction to a workmate, follow God's advice and flee. Stop it. Back off. Distance yourself. A member of a couple after God's own heart has eyes for only one person—his or her marriage partner.

David's Advances (2 Samuel 11:2,4)

David succumbed to temptation by pursuing Bathsheba. But what role did Bathsheba play in all this? Did she bear any responsibility? After all, Bathsheba had elected to bathe where it was possible for her to be seen. Had she been more modest, she probably would have taken measures to keep her bathing more private. Yet at the same time, it's possible she expected the king would be gone in battle. She didn't know he would see her from his rooftop.

And why didn't she refuse David's summons to the palace? It's possible she didn't know David's intent when he sent his messengers to bring her back to him. But when David began making romantic advances to her, nothing is said in Scripture to suggest Bathsheba resisted. Was she lonely or in a loveless marriage? Was she enamored by the king and the thought that he demanded her presence? Was she flattered by David's desire for her? Was she simply afraid to say anything because he was the king? Because there is nothing that indicates she declined David's romantic overtures, there's a possibility she went along willingly.

David's Deadly Solution (2 Samuel 11:5-21)

Whatever the case, the inevitable happened: David and Bathsheba's few hours together may have seemed tender and beautiful to them—or at minimum, to him. Most affairs give this illusion. But in the eyes of God, what had occurred was adultery. It was sin. And it was hideous and ugly.

And to make matters worse, Bathsheba became pregnant.

David's next challenge was how to hide his sin and Bathsheba's pregnancy, especially from Bathsheba's husband. David, the leader of the army and all things military, decided to send for Bathsheba's soldier husband to come home for a little R & R, thinking Uriah would surely want to sleep with Bathsheba.

But her husband was too honorable. Because his fellow soldiers were still fighting on the front, he declared, "Shall I then go to my house to eat and drink, and to lie with my wife?...I will not do this thing" (verse 11). The dedicated soldier-husband, Uriah, would not go along with David's scheme. So, as a last resort, David ordered his general, Joab, to put Uriah at the front of the battle line and withdraw the troops from around him, assuring Uriah's death by the enemy.

In doing this, David added murder to his sin of adultery.

David's Sin Exposed (2 Samuel 12:1-23)

After Bathsheba observed the appropriate period of mourning for her husband, David took her as his wife. And he probably breathed a huge sigh of relief, assuming he had managed to hide his wrongdoings. "But the thing that David had done displeased the LORD" (11:27).

Among Satan's lies about sin are (1) that no one will ever know, and (2) hey, the consequences won't be so bad. Sure, people may not know what you've done, but God knows. And God acts. In David's case, God sent Nathan the prophet to confront David's sin. Sin is costly, and, as a result of David's sin, the child of his affair died.

And the effects of sin are never limited to only those who commit the sins. Sin's consequences can trickle down for generations to come. We see this in David's case. Perhaps because of his ungodly example, David's children were rebellious and committed incest, murder, and treason. Even David's own son, Absalom, tried to have David assassinated. The prophet Nathan had warned David, "The sword shall never depart from your house, because you have despised Me" (12:10). As a consequence of his sin, David no longer experienced peace in his home or family.

Countless people were hurt by David and Bathsheba's transgression. And above all, God was offended. He said, "Why have you despised the commandment of the LORD, to do evil in His sight?…you have despised Me" (12:9-10). David had it all, but for a moment of passion, he lost everything!

David's Confession (2 Samuel 12:13)

In David, we witness a fact of life—no one is perfect, including us! But one of the traits of a man or woman after God's own heart is their willingness to confess their sins. David wasn't perfect, and he refused to acknowledge his sin with Bathsheba for nearly a year. If you read his confession in Psalms 32, 38, and 51, you can sense the guilt and agony his unconfessed sin produced in his heart and soul.

No, David wasn't perfect. But what set him apart from his predecessor, Saul, was his willingness to eventually confess his sin. Saul made excuses. He never saw himself at fault, but always as the victim. By contrast, David fell before the Lord in remorse.

God wants a godly couple. To be that couple, you must each keep a clean slate with God. Willingly admit your failures to Him—and to one another.

David's Forgiveness (2 Samuel 12:13)

With David's confession came blessed forgiveness. David said to Nathan, "I have sinned against the LORD." And Nathan said to David, "The LORD also has put away your sin; you shall not die" (verse 13). Scripture does not tell us, but if Bathsheba was a willing accomplice, surely she also acknowledged her sin and knew God's forgiveness as well. God is gracious and willingly accepts our confession, and joyously offers His forgiveness. While you cannot erase the consequences of sin, you can live in the full assurance of God's complete forgiveness.

David's sin with Bathsheba was a major blemish on his legacy (1 Kings 15:5). But neither he nor Bathsheba let this ruin what remained of their lives. David never married another woman, and Solomon, their second son, was chosen by God as David's successor. God forgave this sinning couple, and they went on. They seem to have forgiven each other and gone on to live in harmony to the end of David's life. And, to add blessing upon blessing, Bathsheba was chosen to be one of the four women mentioned in the genealogy of Christ (Matthew 1:6).

Putting It All Together

The first half of David's life was filled with war and conquest. In his military life, David was a superstar. But in his personal life, he was out of control, and one day, in one act with a woman named Bathsheba, his life and leadership took a wrong turn. Going from bad to worse, David acted to cover up his adultery by murdering Bathsheba's husband, who is labeled by one Bible commentator as "the most loyal of all David's men." [11]

Their sordid story marks a turning point in David's life and the internal state of his kingdom. There were drastic consequences, but with his repentant confession and God's forgiveness, he and Bathsheba picked up the pieces and made the best of their relationship.

And God gave them Solomon, whose name is said to mean "(God Is) His Peace." [12] He became king after David, for the most part ruled wisely, and entered into the messianic line—the line of Christ. The tale of David and Bathsheba is tragic, but with God's grace, they made their marriage work.

This same grace from God is available to you and your spouse. Sin occurs in every marriage, but, like David and Bathsheba, you can repent, confess, and forgive. You can regroup and go on. You can take all the lessons learned through shortcomings and failure, join hands and hearts, and move forward. With God's grace, help, and wisdom, you too can make your marriage work.

• Lessons for Wives from Bathsheba •

1. *Learn to live with a leader.* In spite of how it happened, Bathsheba was married to a leader—to David, a mighty general and king. One of her positive qualities was her ability to be an affirming influence and support to David. As already stated, no other wife is mentioned after David's marriage to Bathsheba. Through the years—and even on his deathbed—David seems to have listened to her. We actually see Nathan, the prophet, delivering a critical message to David through Bathsheba as he lay dying (1 Kings 1:11-18).

Your husband is a leader, too. If he's a husband, he's a leader. If you have children, he's a leader. If he earns an income, he's a leader. Whether in the neighborhood, the workplace, at church, or on a committee or sports team, he's a leader. He doesn't have to be a general or king to be a leader. As a man of God, a man in whom the Spirit of God dwells and empowers, he is a leader. Your job is to encourage and support him in his commitments and responsibilities.

2. *Keep your eyes fixed forward.* Here's some touching, bolstering wisdom for victorious daily living:

> A lesson we can learn from Bathsheba is that being assured of God's forgiveness she did not let her one sin ruin her entire life. Repentant, she used her mistake as a guide to future, better conduct. When we brood over sins God has said He will remember no more

against us, we actually doubt His mercy, and rob ourselves of spiritual power and progress. [13]

Only God will—and can—give you a second chance. Whatever your past, don't bring it into your present. Your relationship with your husband may not have started out much better than Bathsheba's relationship with David, but with God's forgiveness, you can go on. Don't look back; look forward. The future is bright, and God has great plans for you and your husband.

3. *A wife with a mission.* God gave Bathsheba and David a second chance and a second son. To her credit, it appears that Bathsheba determined to be the best wife and mother she could be. Despite the way her marriage to David began, and the sorrow and heartache they had already suffered, she wanted to take advantage of her second chance. One prime way she could and did help her husband was to prepare Solomon, the son who was later born to the two of them, for kingly leadership. In the Bible text, we don't read much about Bathsheba until David is on his deathbed and Solomon is a grown man. But we know she was busy during those silent years. She was behind the scenes, quietly and systematically raising Solomon, training him, loving him, and grooming him. One day he would be king, and she wanted him to be ready and confident.

And train him she did! She dedicated herself to diligently do as Solomon himself later wrote in Proverbs 22:6—train up [Solomon] in the way he should go. Tradition says that it was Bathsheba who wrote Proverbs 31 to help prepare Solomon to lead from the throne (Proverbs 31:1-9) and to find an excellent wife (verses 10-31). It's no wonder that Solomon became the wisest man on earth and a great king. His vast wisdom and love for God was very likely a reflection of her own spiritual condition.

Your mission is to be there for your husband, right beside him in body, heart, and soul, through thick and thin, to assist him in being a leader in the home the two of you are building. Be a support for him on his job, and an encourager in all things. And if or when you have children, do your part to raise the children to love God, love their dad, love their family, serve others, walk wisely, and be a positive and productive member of society. That's your mission—a mission that matters.

4. *Modesty is a must.* How did Bathsheba end up in an improper, immoral, unlawful relationship with David? She was careless in her behavior—she made herself immodest in a highly visible location. As a result, Bathsheba, along with David, was plunged into sin and sorrow. It was a costly choice on her part because ultimately it led to the loss of her husband, Uriah, and her baby by David.

Modesty will never go out of style. God requires it of his women—past, present, and future. Don't succumb to the fashion standards set by your culture. Sure, be stylish, but be modest. And be sure to teach your daughters modesty as well. The best way to do that? Model it for them. As a woman, wife, and mom after God's own heart, hold to His standard. It will bring honor to your husband and glory to the Lord. What more could you want?

• Lessons for Husbands from David •

1. *Obedience is the key to life—and marriage.* With all we see from this chapter on the life of David, it would be hard to spot the quality of obedience in him. Yet God tells us in Acts 13:22, "I have found David the son of Jesse, a man after My own heart, who will do all My will." In spite of David's grievous wrongdoing, obedience was still the dominant trait in his life. And when he was confronted with his sin, he repented.

This shining trait in David's heart should be what you as a husband desire. You already know you are not perfect, nor is it possible to be. But you can continue to make progress toward spiritual maturity and usefulness. And how do you progress? How do you move forward and grow? Read God's Word. Obey God's Word. And when you sin, confess it quickly. These steps will keep you on the fast track to being a man and husband after God's own heart.

2. *Gaze only on your wife.* David had a problem with women. He was very human, and in today's culture he would be considered a womanizer. Women were his major area of weakness. How do we know this? God's law instructed kings not to multiply wives, lest they turn his heart away from God (Deuteronomy 17:17). Yet David disregarded this. He had six wives before he married Bathsheba, and that doesn't even include all of his concubines (2 Samuel 5:13)!

Instead of following God's law, David followed the example of other Oriental kings by having a harem as a display of his wealth and power. David let his culture influence him to go ahead and fulfill his lustful passions, disregarding the perfect will of God—one woman for one man.

Thank God for the wife He has given you. Love her. Adore her. Spoil her. Kiss her. Be a one-woman man who has eyes only for his wife.

3. *Check your armor for cracks.* David had a problem—a crack in his spiritual armor—and that problem was lust. What are the cracks in your armor? You already know your areas of weakness... and so does God. So why not admit them? Why not confess them to the Lord? Why not deal with them? And why not do as the Bible commands so many times and "put away" your secret sin? Don't let a small crack in your armor turn into a sin that will reap major consequences.

4. *Confess your sin quickly.* David was God's man—both before he knew Bathsheba and afterward. But he had an in-between time

when he had a problem with confessing sin. David wanted what he wanted—Bathsheba—and he took what he wanted. He committed adultery and orchestrated the death of Bathsheba's loyal husband. Suddenly David's steady stream of repentant prayers stopped. He ceased lifting up his failures to God for forgiveness. He—and his heart—went silent. David stubbornly held on to his sin for almost a year—until his child with Bathsheba died. Later he described his physical condition during that long year when his heart was hardened against the Lord:

> When I kept silent, my bones grew old through my groaning all the day long. For day and night Your hand was heavy upon me; my vitality was turned into the drought of summer. I acknowledged my sin to You, and my iniquity I have not hidden. I said, "I will confess my transgressions to the LORD," and You forgave the iniquity of my sin (Psalm 32:3-5).

As the spiritual leader in your marriage and home, keep the pathway to God open. Use a part of your daily prayer time searching your heart, taking care of sin, receiving God's forgiveness, and rejoicing in His love. Imagine the difference these few minutes of honesty with God will make in you—and in your relationship with your wife!

5. *Be a husband after God's own heart.* Looking back over David's marriages, and especially his marriage to Bathsheba, we can't help but shake our heads, and pray, "Please, God, don't let that be me!" But a handful of overarching truths woven through David's life do emerge to help you—and me—be a husband after God's own heart.

Love. True love for your wife begins with a vibrant love for God and His Word. A husband after God's own heart commits to following God with all his heart, soul, mind, and strength. Your wife is blessed when you are that man.

Learn. Your Bible is the ultimate gold mine of information. Between its covers you will find truth, wisdom, instruction, and inspiration from God's heart to yours. Add to that some godly mentoring, and you should be well on your way to being a better husband, and ready for the next step God has in mind for you and your family.

Lead. As a married man, you have someone to lead—your wonderful wife! And as a man after God's own heart, you have the strength and power to become a leader in every facet of your life.

Live. Every day, just one day at a time, determine to really live. God's future for you is not yet revealed. And your past is gone—and forgiven. So His will for you today is in the present. In the words of missionary and martyr Jim Elliot, "Wherever you are, be all there. Live to the hilt every situation you believe to be the will of God."

Building a Marriage that Lasts

David and Bathsheba. Even today as you read these two names your first thought is probably negative and judgmental. "Oh, yeah, I've heard of them! David committed adultery with her and had her husband killed." But before your negative thoughts go too far, think about the lesson their example sends to you these 3000-plus years later.

They were a couple that messed up—in a large, appalling way. But they also did the right thing about their sin. They admitted their wrongs, fell on God's grace, and received His merciful and compassionate forgiveness.

And they are a couple who, in all humility, accepted God's forgiveness. He, the God of the universe, extended to them a gracious, full-of-life second chance. And they grabbed onto it. There's no doubt about the heartbreaking consequences and fallout from sin that followed David and Bathsheba all the days of their lives. But, to their credit, they picked themselves up, joined together, and went on.

Things that require forgiveness will happen in your marriage relationship. And things that require forgiveness have already happened in your marriage relationship. God's prescription for past, present, and future failures is always the same—you are to forgive. Large or small, any and all offenses must be forgiven.

David and Bathsheba's experience is speaking to you right now, as a couple, today. God does not reveal all the details about how David and Bathsheba worked out their issues and dealt with forgiving one another, but you do know exactly what God tells you to do today to work out forgiveness in your marriage—you are to forgive, period. In fact, it's commanded. Take these instructions from God's Word to heart. But more than that, do it:

> As the elect of God, holy and beloved, put on tender mercies, kindness, humility, meekness, long-suffering; bearing with one another, and forgiving one other, if anyone has a complaint against another; even as Christ forgave you, so you also must do. But above all these things put on love, which is the bond of perfection (Colossians 3:12-14).
>
> Let all bitterness, wrath, anger, clamor, and evil speaking be put away from you, with all malice. And be kind to one another, tenderhearted, forgiving one another, even as God in Christ forgave you (Ephesians 4:31-32).

8

Zacharias and Elizabeth

Partners with Pure Hearts

They were both righteous before God,
walking in all the commandments
and ordinances of the Lord blameless.

LUKE 1:6

As Elizabeth went about her daily duties around the home she shared with her husband of many years, she couldn't stop thinking about him. He was so precious to her, her constant companion, her one-and-only true love—her best friend. Zacharias had been gone for only two days, and there were still five days to go. No, she knew seven days wasn't a long time, and it didn't happen often. Her husband had to be gone only one week out of every six months. She was honored to be married to a man from the priestly order. Zacharias not only held the office of priest, but he lived the life of a priest. He was kind, generous, godly, loving, and, most important of all, supportive of her predicament—a predicament that caused her to be a public disgrace.

Elizabeth was barren.

All the other wives in the village had children galore. Children upon children! And now their children were having children. She could see their joy through her own sorrow-filled eyes as she faithfully went to the well and shopped in the marketplace to care for the two of them—Zacharias and herself.

Yes, being barren was considered a divine curse in the Jewish culture where this couple after God's own heart lived. And Elizabeth has been on the receiving end of this scorn for decades!

Yet she and Zacharias hadn't given up hope. Elizabeth was comforted by the fact that others like Sarah, Rebekah, Rachel, and Hannah had also been barren, yet God had intervened, and they had conceived and borne children—children who had grown up to become patriarchs and priests in their own right.

Elizabeth held onto hope and continued to trust God. She tried hard not to think about the fact that she was getting beyond childbearing age—that time was running out...if it hadn't already.

And then there was Zacharias. How she wished he would stop talking about being an old man. That scared her and dampened her dream of having a baby. In her eyes, she would always see him as the handsome young man at their wedding celebration.

But throughout their many years of shame, bewilderment, and heartache, both Elizabeth and Zacharias sought with all their hearts to live uprightly in the sight of God, to carefully observe the Lord's commandments and regulations, to please the God of their fathers. This didn't mean they were sinless. But they were intent on faithfully following God's will and ways as dictated by the Law and the Prophets. With hearts like theirs, it's obvious, contrary to the people's conclusions, this couple was experiencing childlessness because of physical problems, not spiritual ones.

As Elizabeth again got lost in her thoughts, little did she realize that the stage was set for a miracle. This sweet, devoted couple's condition was about to serve as a spectacular opportunity for God to display His direct control in the affairs of men. With God's supernatural assistance, as with other couples in the past, God would, in His perfect timing, provide a child for this godly couple. And not just a child, but a child who would prepare the way for the long-awaited Messiah.

What's Going On?

Zacharias and Elizabeth provide an outstanding example of what it looks like to be a couple after God's own heart, and what a couple's obedience to God looks like in real, everyday life. Here's what we know about this couple who lived in the hill country of Judah so many centuries ago.

A Uncommon Couple (Luke 1:5-7)

Can you imagine being able to trace your lineage back thousands of years? Well, this latest couple after God's own heart could do just that. They were both from the priestly line of Aaron, Moses' brother and the first high priest of Israel. And, in addition to their prestigious pedigree, God gives an astounding evaluation of their character: They were both righteous before God (Luke 1:6).

Like Adam and Eve, who initially walked with God in the cool of the day and obeyed His commands, Zacharias and Elizabeth also lived obediently, walking in all the commandments and ordinances of the Lord (Luke 1:6). As a result God prepared to use them as His instruments to provide the messenger who would announce the coming of God's Son, the Messiah. Light is about to enter darkness!

A Unique Opportunity (Luke 1:8-10)

We first meet Zacharias while he is burning incense just outside the veil that divided the holy place from the Most Holy Place. Luke recorded that Zacharias's division was on duty. This division was one of 24 groups of priests, drawn up and organized by King David (1 Chronicles 24:7-18). The priests in each division were on duty twice a year for a week at a time. Zacharias had served in a variety of roles at the temple twice a year for years. But this time was different. This time he was chosen by lot, out of all the officiating priests, for a special task.

Zacharias knew exactly what he was to do. He had trained all his life for this one opportunity. The incense for which Zacharias was responsible symbolized the prayers of the entire nation of Israel. Therefore, at that particular moment, Zacharias was the focal point of the entire Jewish nation as the worshippers prayed outside the temple and waited for him to finish the offering.

An Unusual Visitor (Luke 1:11-17)

Alone with his own thoughts and prayers as he prepared the incense for the altar, Zacharias was utterly shocked by what appeared—or should we say *who* appeared! He saw the angel Gabriel standing at the right side of the altar (verse 11)! Responding as anyone in his right mind would at the sight of a celestial being, Zacharias was afraid. But the angel calmed him with some good news, saying, "Do not be afraid, Zacharias, for your prayer is heard; and your wife Elizabeth will bear you a son, and you shall call his name John" (verse 13). Then Gabriel went on to detail six roles that Zacharias's son John would fulfill during his lifetime (verses 14-17).

An Unbelieving Reaction (Luke 1:18-22)

Zacharias had doubts that he and Elizabeth could have a son. After all, both of them were old. But the angel identified himself as "Gabriel, who stands in the presence of God, and was sent to speak to you and bring you these glad tidings" (verse 19). He reassured Zacharias that this good news was from the Lord.

From the moment Zacharias questioned the angel in unbelief, he was unable to speak, which was, to some degree, a punishment for his unbelief. But it was also a sign which, in the Old Testament, often accompanied a word of prophecy. For the next nine months, Zacharias's attempts to speak would prove the reality of Gabriel's message.

When Zacharias finally came out of the temple, he could only communicate by motioning with his hands. The people waiting outside came to realize that a miracle had occurred, that Zacharias had seen a vision.

An Uplifting Response (Luke 1:23-25)

After completing his temple duty, a mute Zacharias returned home to Judah's hill country. As predicted by the angel Gabriel, Elizabeth became pregnant and stayed in seclusion for five months. In the silence of her private retreat, Elizabeth acknowledged her joy at finally being able to have a baby. Unlike her husband, she responded with complete assurance that God was the source of her joy: "Thus the Lord has dealt with me, in the days when He looked on me, to take away my reproach among people" (verse 25). At the time, Elizabeth did not indicate that she knew anything about the destiny of her son. However, because she, even before Zacharias was able to speak, knew that the baby's name was to be John (verse 60), Zacharias had probably communicated his entire vision to Elizabeth in writing.

An Unexpected Blessing (Luke 1:39-45)

As God's Word has already informed us, Elizabeth was a righteous and blameless woman. But she soon experienced what few Old Testament saints experienced—she was filled with the Holy Spirit when she was visited by her cousin Mary. With the guidance of God, Elizabeth stated some incredible things about her young cousin, Mary, when Mary entered Elizabeth's house. Elizabeth perceived what was happening to Mary—that she was pregnant, that God's plan for the salvation of mankind was in motion, and that Mary had been assigned a special blessing in giving birth to God's Son, the Messiah, Jesus Christ the Lord.

An Unrehearsed Speech (Luke 1:67-79)

At last, Elizabeth's time arrived and she gave birth to a son, just as the angel Gabriel had prophesied. When the people asked for the baby's name, she replied, "John" (verse 60). The crowd thought this was a highly unusual response. Why, shouldn't the boy be named after his father or a relative? Why John? Where did that come from?

They then asked Zacharias about the boy's name, and he confirmed Elizabeth's reply by writing on a tablet, "His name is John" (verse 63). Immediately—and miraculously—Zacharias's voice returned. In awe, the people knew something wondrous was happening. Zacharias, like Elizabeth, was filled with the Holy Spirit and uttered a marvelous prophecy about God's promise of salvation for the nation. He revealed that this child, John, would be called "the prophet of the Highest; for [he] will go before the face of the Lord to prepare His ways, to give knowledge of salvation to His people by the remission of their sins" (verses 76-77).

Putting It All Together

Picture this: It has been 400 years since God last spoke to man. In a backwater part of Israel, a godly but barren couple named Zacharias and Elizabeth are about to be rewarded for their love and devotion. Sure, there was love and devotion for one another. But greater than that, there was love and devotion in both their hearts for God.

God, in His timing, sent His angel Gabriel with glad tidings of the soon arrival of the forerunner—the herald—for the Messiah. Gabriel brought the news of a son to the priest, Zacharias. Gabriel privately appeared to Zacharias while he was performing his duties in the temple at the altar of incense. With no one else present, Gabriel described the world-changing events that were about to take place.

Maybe Zacharias's age or his long years of disappointment weighed on him, but for whatever reason, he voiced doubt to the angel sent from God. He wondered how he and Elizabeth could possibly have a baby at this stage of their lives. First, Gabriel assured him that the message was true because it came straight from the mouth of God Himself. Then he announced that Zacharias would be mute until the child's birth. God's Word was soon validated when Elizabeth became pregnant.

Elizabeth and Zacharias, a couple who had spent their entire adult lives devoted to obeying God's commands, now had only nine months to prepare for the arrival and training of this special child. This couple after God's own heart, these partners in purity, became—just as God had promised through His messenger, the angel Gabriel—parents of God's messenger for His Son. Jesus gave this tribute and evaluation of their son, John: "Among those born of women there has not risen one greater than John the Baptist" (Matthew 11:11).

• Lessons for Wives from Elizabeth •

1. *Your dreams don't always come true.* Elizabeth was a blessed woman. To begin her list of blessings, she was a daughter of a priest of Israel. She could trace her lineage back to Aaron, the first high priest of Israel. In fact, she bore the name of Aaron's own wife, Elisheba or Elizabeth, which means "God is my oath." And she had married a respected priest. Everyone had predicted a long life with many children for this special couple. But sadly, real life hadn't turned out as predicted. And instead of seeing her as blessed, the religious community saw Elizabeth's barrenness as a curse from God.

How is life turning out for you? Maybe your dreams are all coming true, or maybe you feel like you're still waiting for life to get started. Maybe you feel like there's too much pain and disillusionment to handle. Life has a way of putting detours, roadblocks, and immovable barriers in your path. This was Elizabeth's story—a life of dashed dreams. But rather than have a pity party, Elizabeth chose to gain spiritual strength from her condition. She refused to allow her sorrow to drag her down. Instead, she reached out to grab hold of God's strength.

How do you cope with discouragement, disappointment, adversity, and dashed dreams? Take a lesson from Elizabeth, whose name means "God is my oath." No matter what your situation, look to God for strength each day. A woman after God's own heart does not look at the day's problems; she looks at the power of her God to assist her with those problems! Like Elizabeth, cling to God, whatever your circumstance.

2. *You can rise above bad circumstances.* Proverbs 31:12 tells us that a virtuous wife "does [her husband] good and not evil all the days of her life." As a woman who was called "blameless" by God, Elizabeth was that virtuous wife. The stigma of barrenness had to have weighed heavily on her. This burden could have affected her personality and attitude. It would have been easy for her to sink into depression, despair, and discouragement. But Elizabeth didn't. She sought to live a pure life according to the Law, to be a "blameless" wife, to soar in the joy of the Lord in spite of her situation.

Elizabeth's life response to adversity was a "God thing." Only God could produce contentment and peace in her life circumstances. When your strength is waning, when you sense sadness or despair creeping into your soul, look to God's Word. It will give you abundant strength to face discouragement and adversities day by day. God's Word will light up your dark path of despair and disappointment. There's no need to get lost in a dark hole of hopelessness. Follow the light to productivity and peace of mind—to hope.

3. *It's always possible to grow spiritually.* Elizabeth endured years of scorn from her community. How could she have weathered the ridicule? Luke 1:6 answers that for us: She walked "in all the

commandments and ordinances of the Lord," which meant she was blameless. She didn't succumb to jealousy, or lash out, retaliate, try to defend herself or set the people straight, or spend hours each day thinking of ways to get even with her tormentors. She didn't blame Zacharias, and she didn't blame God, walk away from Him, or give up.

No, Elizabeth chose to spend the hours of her day drawing near to God, refusing to worry about what she didn't have, and focusing on what she did have. She didn't care what the people were thinking about her, but she sure cared what God thought about her! Her heart was devoted to living for God and according to His Word.

Elizabeth was an amazing woman and a wife after God's own heart. She matched her husband, the priest, with her own spiritual maturity...which is a good word for all Christian wives! Even in marriage and maybe as a result of marriage, you need to be purposefully growing spiritually.

You cannot control your husband's growth, but you can control yours. What will that growth produce in you? You will become a wife who walks by the Spirit. A wife filled with God's love, joy, peace, patience, kindness, goodness, faithfulness, gentleness, and self-control—His fruit of the Spirit (Galatians 5:22-23). You do your part to be blameless, and pray that your husband will want to follow Zacharias's example in his walk with God.

4. *First things first.* Do you realize that the time you spend reading and studying God's Word and kneeling in devoted prayer are holy times of preparation, not only for yourself, but for ministry to others? And that ministry starts right in your own home. The effectiveness of your ministry to your husband and children and to others will be in direct proportion to the time you spend away from people and with God in a daily quiet time of preparation. Others who need help or encouragement will be drawn to your godly influence.

What kind of others? Maybe others like…Mary! While the angel Gabriel was telling Mary that she would bring the Savior into the world, he informed her that her relative, Elizabeth, was also going to have a baby. With no one around who could help her understand what was happening, Mary went on a road trip to see Elizabeth. As a godly "older woman," Elizabeth would definitely have wisdom to offer Mary, a teenager. Sparks flew as these two blessed, committed-to-the-Lord women sat down together and blessed one another, magnified the Lord, and affirmed their roles in God's plan.

• Lessons for Husbands from Zacharias •

1. *It's all about your heart.* As a Christian man and husband, you want godliness to be the foremost quality in your life, right? So Zacharias, a man of God, provides clues about how you can be a man and husband after God's own heart. Here's how Zacharias's heart and inner life are described: He was righteous before God, and he was "blameless" (Luke 1:6).

Many husbands appear righteous in the public eye, and especially at church. They play the "church game" extremely well. They profess faith in Christ and *display* all the outward activities of godliness. But they fail in the sight of God. They are not blameless in their daily life—nor are they even trying to be. Zacharias, however, walked with God on a daily basis—for decades, even well into his senior years…until the day he walked right into heaven!

You might be wondering, *How was he able to do this? And if he could do it, why can't I? What does it take? Am I up for it?*

Zacharias shows you what's needed. He was devoted to obeying God's Word. The Bible says Zacharias spent his life walking "in all the commandments and ordinances of the Lord blameless" (1:6). This man didn't just carry out some of the laws of God. It says *all.* Today we would say Zacharias would qualify as a

New Testament elder or leader, one who must be "above reproach" (1 Timothy 3:2 NASB).

So what does it take to be a man after God's own heart? It takes a working knowledge of God's Word. It takes studying that Word. And it takes a deep desire to obey that Word. God does not set impossible standards for His people. His Word says a man can be blameless, and Zacharias modeled the standard for you.

2. *Marriage is for better or worse.* We've already noted that Zacharias and Elizabeth experienced the social stigma of having no children, an issue for many of the couples we've looked at in this book. These couples teach us that there will always be some kind of trial that weighs a marriage down. There will always be some issue or nagging problem that can cause long-term difficulties. Just one ongoing problem can drain the life and vitality out of your marriage.

But Zacharias and Elizabeth break the mold for us. They carried the emotional burden of infertility for as long as they had been married. And yet amazingly the Bible declares that they were both righteous before God. This couple refused to allow any adverse circumstances to affect their relationship with God and their love for each other.

How about you? Are you a Zacharias, a husband who hangs in there loving his wife, no matter what? "For better or for worse"? You probably thought your wife was practically perfect when you married her, that she would be the ideal life partner for you. So wouldn't godly love continue to see her as perfect? No matter how long you and your wife have been married, or what happens along the way, you can love her. Righteousness demands your selfless love.

3. *Commit to praying for your wife.* You would expect a godly husband to pray faithfully for his wife, wouldn't you? Especially if he knew there was a deep burden she was carrying day after day.

Zacharias did. When the angel Gabriel spoke to Zacharias, he said, "Do not be afraid, Zacharias, for your prayer is heard; and your wife Elizabeth will bear you a son, and you shall call his name John" (Luke 1:13). It's obvious from the angel's words that Zacharias had prayed for Elizabeth to bear a child. He may have been praying for this very thing for years, and he may have been praying for it while he stood where the angel found him, right there before the altar while tending his priestly duties. Zacharias's prayers for his wife are a model for your mission as a husband.

Do you want to be a more caring and loving husband? Then your first assignment is to determine the Number One burden, challenge, or heartache your wife is dealing with, and then faithfully pray for her. Maybe you know what it is, and you just haven't been as faithful as you should be to present her difficult life-situation to God for His help. So now is definitely the time to start. And if you don't know what her problem is, ask her...and then commit to diligently praying for her regarding this matter. Imagine what it will mean to her to know that you are joining with her to carry her greatest struggle...together. And to top it off, to know that at least one person—the most important person in her life, you!—is faithfully presenting her problem to the loving, all-powerful God of the universe for His help.

4. *Be faithful in all things, large and small.* Do you ever feel like your job is boring, insignificant, and fruitless? If anyone might have thought their occupation was a little dull, it could have been Zacharias. It is estimated there were at least 1000 priests in each of the 24 divisions that serviced the temple. You do the math—that's 24,000 priests, and each one served only two weeks per year in the temple. Now for some more math: That means each priest waited around for 50 weeks just to do his job. It was a significant job, and a huge privilege, but with that many priests and all the downtime, some of them might have felt their job was a tad insignificant.

But again, Zacharias was not your typical guy. He realized he was serving God, regardless of what role he was given, regardless of waiting for his date-of-service to roll around. Yet God greatly honored Zacharias's faithfulness as he was one of the select few who were ever chosen to offer up incense in the Most Holy Place. You can clearly see a powerful model of faithfulness in this humble priest.

Faithfulness is required of you too. Here's why: You, as God's servant, are to be found faithful (1 Corinthians 4:2). You are to be faithful in word and deed (Colossians 3:17). And faithfulness is a fruit of the Spirit (Galatians 5:22). Bottom line? Faithfulness is a godly quality. So be faithful on your job. But at the same time, don't neglect to be faithful to nurture your wife and family in the things of God. Be faithful to provide for your family—and be especially faithful to your vows to love, cherish, and honor your wife.

Building a Marriage that Lasts

I have to say that my wife, Elizabeth, truly understands and lives her roles and responsibilities as a wife. And I thank God that she desires to be a woman and wife after God's own heart. But still, I can't force her to read her Bible, pray, go to church, or be part of a Bible study. She must make those decisions herself. Sure, I can pray, hint, suggest, and encourage her, but in the end, Elizabeth must have the inner desire to grow.

And the same applies regarding me. Elizabeth can't make me grow as a Christian man, husband, or spiritual leader. I have to want to grow.

The same applies to you and your wife. Neither of you can make the other grow or want to grow in the things of the Lord. So what can a couple do?

First, *talk*! Talk about it. Just as communication is the key to your marriage, it is a key to setting a plan for growth. Talk about what each of you is or isn't doing in the spiritual growth department. Then talk about what you wish would happen, what you think it would take to grow. Talk about what kinds of materials you could use and tools that would help (maybe a Bible with study notes, a Bible reading plan, a devotional on the names or attributes of God, or the life of Christ, that you can read together). You are a unique couple, so aim for a plan that works well for the two of you.

Your ultimate goal is that both of you—as husband and wife—commit to keep growing spiritually. And this is where the challenge starts. A commitment to grow, and to do it together, is a huge step. So do whatever it takes. Consider making a pact. Maybe you could even write out a pledge to each other.

And factor in a few fun things in your new joint effort! Set up a weekly date to talk about your week, what you learned, where you struggled, changes you've seen in yourself and in each other. One couple Elizabeth and I know have gone to a fast-food eatery for a baked potato every Wednesday night—for 30 years! It's a standing, forever date they both relish. Again, do whatever it takes to solidify and encourage your mutual desire to grow spiritually.

Your decision and commitment to focus on growing in Christ will be a major step that moves you forward in your quest to become a couple after God's own heart. Without this keen focus on growing in maturity, you'll have trouble sustaining your walk with God individually and especially as a couple. Everything beyond this starting point with God as the joint focus in your lives and your marriage will then be built on a strong relationship with God. Remember, the theme verse for this chapter stated that Zacharias and Elizabeth "were both righteous before God, [both] walking in all the commandments and ordinances of the Lord [both] blameless" (Luke 1:6).

Here's a project for you: Pray over this verse and then put your names in the blanks below. Wouldn't you like this to be an epitaph and summary statement commemorating your lives as a couple—maybe even on your tombstones? It's a thought!

_____ and _____
were both righteous before God,
both walking in all the commandments
and ordinances of the Lord,
both blameless.

9

Joseph and Mary

A Couple in Crisis

When Mary had been betrothed to
Joseph, before they came together
she was found to be with child by the Holy Spirit.
And Joseph her husband, being a righteous man
and not wanting to disgrace her,
planned to send her away secretly.

MATTHEW 1:18-19 (NASB)

"Thank You, Lord, for another fantastic day!" Joseph exclaimed as he opened the doors of his combination home/workshop. Joseph was on top of the world. He had been trained in a useful trade by his father, a trade that he hoped to pass on to a son of his own in the future.

A son of his own. Joseph grinned as his thoughts went immediately to his betrothed, Mary. Years ago, their parents made arrangements for the two of them to be married when the time was right. And that time was fast approaching. Life was short and couples, at least the women, married young. Mary had just reached a marriage-able age, and plans for the wedding were in full swing.

Joseph was excited today because his Mary was on her way back from a visit with her cousin Elizabeth, and he was going to finally see her. It had been three whole months since Mary had left Nazareth. Joseph couldn't wait for his beloved bride to return.

But hey, it would be a while before Mary arrived. So to pass the time, Joseph headed for his shop so he could work on a piece of furniture for their future home together.

What's Going On?

In Scripture, two couples stand out as noble products of an Old Testament Jewish upbringing. We met the first couple in the previous chapter—Zacharias and Elizabeth. And now we are immediately drawn into the story of the second couple—Joseph and Mary. This husband and wife will play an even more significant role in the events surrounding the birth and ministry of the Savior of the world, Jesus Christ.

The Angelic Announcement (Luke 1:26-38)

One day during Joseph and Mary's betrothal period—that is, their engagement—Mary received a visit from the angel Gabriel. The angel told Mary, "You will conceive in your womb and bring forth a Son, and shall call His name JESUS" (verse 31). This announcement presented a bit of a problem. Because Mary had not yet married, she was still a virgin. How was she supposed to conceive? But she didn't dismiss the news. Instead, she submitted willingly to God's plan, saying, "Behold the maidservant of the Lord! Let it be to me according to your word" (verse 38).

However, Mary's obedience to the call of God on her life would later present a crisis. When Joseph, who didn't yet know of God's plan, became aware that Mary was pregnant, he wondered if he should bring an end to their betrothal.

Affirmation from Elizabeth (Luke 1:36-56)

Mary was probably around 14 years old when she received the news from Gabriel. After Gabriel announced that Mary would give birth to Jesus, he also mentioned, "Elizabeth your relative has also conceived a son in her old age; and this is now the sixth month for her who was called barren. For with God nothing will be impossible" (Luke 1:36-37).

With this information about Elizabeth, and before anyone else in the village would know about her condition, including Joseph, Mary quickly left Nazareth to visit her older cousin Elizabeth, who lived some distance away. She stayed with Elizabeth for three months. The Gospel of Luke gives us the account of Mary's time with Elizabeth, and how Elizabeth's understanding, fellowship, and spiritual insights helped Mary in the early days of her pregnancy.

> And it happened, when Elizabeth heard the greeting of Mary, that the babe leaped in her womb; and Elizabeth was filled with the Holy Spirit. Then she spoke out with a loud voice and said, "Blessed are you among women, and blessed is the fruit of your womb! But why is this granted to me, that the mother of my Lord should come to me?" (Luke 1:41-43).

Elizabeth and Zacharias had just experienced God's grace in their lives and the gift of a child on the way—their own miracle baby. Who would be better able to help the young Mary comprehend the incomprehensible? As a result, Mary uttered Spirit-filled praise and adoration of God and the coming Messiah in what many refer to as Mary's Magnificat, found in verses 46-55.

Crisis #1, Dream #1 (Matthew 1:18-25)

Mary stayed with Elizabeth for three months (Luke 1:56), then returned to her hometown, family, and Joseph. That's when Crisis

#1 occurred. How Joseph learned about Mary's pregnancy, we don't know. But we do know that Joseph was a righteous man of God, and he was well acquainted with God's Law. The Bible tells us what Joseph decided to do about Mary: "Joseph her husband, being a righteous man and not wanting to disgrace her, planned to send her away secretly" (Luke 1:19 NASB).

But that night, before Joseph could act on his decision, he received the first of four dreams (Matthew 1:20-25). What message did an angel of the Lord have for him through his dream?

> *He was told of Mary's purity*—"Joseph, son of David, do not be afraid to take to you Mary your wife, for that which is conceived in her is of the Holy Spirit" (verse 20).
>
> *He was told of the Person within Mary*—"She will bring forth a Son, and you shall call His name JESUS" (verse 21).
>
> *He was told of the child's mission*—"He will save His people from their sins" (verse 21).
>
> *He was told of the prophecy about Mary*—"All this was done that it might be fulfilled which was spoken by the Lord through the prophet, saying: 'Behold, the virgin shall be with child, and bear a Son, and they shall call His name Immanuel,' which is translated, 'God with us'" (verses 22-23).

Joseph and Mary got married immediately following this dream. He took her to be his wife and they would not have intercourse until after the birth of Jesus (verses 24-25). Shortly before Jesus' birth, this new couple after God's own heart traveled to Bethlehem to register for the Roman government's required census. While they were in Bethlehem, Jesus Christ, the Savior of the world, was born (Luke 2:1-7).

Crisis #2, Dream #2 (Matthew 2:13-15)

We don't know how long Joseph and Mary stayed in Bethlehem after the birth of Jesus, but by the time the wise men from the East arrived there, the family was staying in a "house" (Matthew 2:11). The wise men, or magi, had followed the star that heralded Jesus' arrival and stopped in Jerusalem, seeking answers from the religious leaders about "where the Christ was to be born" (verse 4). These travelers explained they had "seen His star in the East and [had] come to worship Him" (verse 2).

Unfortunately, their visit ignited the evil paranoia of King Herod. He suddenly wanted to know more about this "star" and about this "Ruler who will shepherd My people Israel" (verses 2,6; see also Micah 5:2). Evidently he was afraid this ruler might usurp his throne.

After the magi were told that, according to a prophecy in Micah 5:2, Jesus would be born in Bethlehem, they traveled onward to that little town. This led to Crisis #2, which led to Dream #2: Joseph was warned by God that Herod would try to kill Jesus, and that he was to flee with his family to Egypt. As with the first dream, Joseph immediately did as he was told: "When he arose, he took the young Child and His mother by night and departed for Egypt, and was there until the death of Herod" (Matthew 2:14).

Crisis #3, Dream #3 (Matthew 2:19-21)

Thanks to the expensive gifts provided by the magi, Joseph, Mary, and the child were able to head south to Egypt and away from the region controlled by Herod. In his anger over being deceived by the magi, Herod created a national crisis by issuing orders to kill all male children up to age two who resided in and around Bethlehem, thinking this would surely eliminate the threat to his kingdom. Now comes Crisis #3 and Dream #3. Joseph, Mary, and Jesus' stay in Egypt lasted until the Lord appeared in a dream to Joseph, saying, "Arise, take the young Child and His mother, and go to the land of Israel, for those who sought the young Child's life are dead" (verse 20). The crisis was that it was time for another move! Moves are always a crisis—even today, and even when things are good. In other words, "Pack it up! It's time to move!"

Crisis #4, Dream #4 (Matthew 2:22-23)

As Joseph led Mary and Jesus back into Israel, Joseph was informed that Archelaus, Herod's son, was ruling in his father's place. Joseph, the protector, went on full crisis alert, fearing for the safety of his family. But this time God Himself came to the rescue in a fourth and final dream. The outcome? "Being warned by God in a dream, [Joseph] turned aside into the region of Galilee. And he came and dwelt in a city called Nazareth" (verse 22).

Putting It All Together

What happened to Mary is a marvelous story of trust and submission. When it comes to Mary, songs are sung, paintings are commissioned, and, in some circles, she is even worshipped. But humble Mary would be the first to say all the praise should go to God alone. She was just a young girl who was obedient to the call of God and willing to submit to whatever He asked of her.

And what about Joseph? He doesn't get anywhere near the attention Mary does. Yet his gracious humility is evident in all that he does as well. And, like Mary, he had a strong trust in God. He listened to God and took Mary as his wife, even though he knew that others in their community would look upon them with suspicion, wondering how Mary had gotten pregnant before they were married. We are told in Scripture that each time Joseph had a dream from God, he immediately obeyed the instructions imparted to him. He, along with Mary, never questioned God's demands on their lives.

Do you remember God's definition of what it means to be a man or woman after God's own heart? It means being a person "who will do all [God's] will" (Acts 13:22). Full obedience to whatever

God required is what prepared Joseph and Mary to take their place in biblical history.

• Lessons for Wives from Mary •

Mary was an adolescent Jewish girl probably in her mid-teens. She was of the tribe of Judah and of the royal line of David. And, as was the custom for girls her age, she was engaged to a local man named Joseph, who was also in the ancestral line of David.

Mary was an amazing young woman who quickly became an amazing wife. Most of what we know about her marriage to Joseph comes from the events surrounding the birth of her son Jesus. Through the brief glimpses into her life as a wife, you can draw at least four principles that will help you live as a wife after God's own heart.

1. *Respond positively to the will of God.* Mary was told that she would have a baby by the Holy Spirit. Her response, even though she didn't understand how this could possibly happen, was one of humble submission. Out of her mouth and heart Mary uttered, "Behold the maidservant of the Lord! Let it be to me according to your word" (Luke 1:38).

As you well know, sometimes it's a challenge to figure out the will of God. But for a wife, God's plan is quite simple. It consists of four tasks: A wife is to help her husband (Genesis 2:18), to follow her husband (Ephesians 5:22), to respect her husband (Ephesians 5:33), and to love her husband (Titus 2:4).

How are you doing at these four tasks? Are you responding positively to God's will for you as a wife? God will honor your efforts when you take His Word to heart. And there's no way to measure how thrilled your husband will be!

2. *Hide God's Word in your heart.* Mary's encounter with the

angel Gabriel lasted only minutes, but the consequences of what he announced to her would endure for eternity. Young Mary showed uncommon maturity. She didn't panic at the appearance of the angel. She didn't run around screaming her head off when she was given the news about bearing and giving birth to Jesus. Rather, she logically and calmly questioned the mechanics of what was to happen to her by asking, "How can this be, since I do not know a man?" (Luke 1:34).

Later, when Mary visited her relative Elizabeth, we again see the depth of Mary's spiritual maturity and its source—she knew God's Word and had stored it up in her heart. Mary's heart overflowed in a song of praise when she arrived at Elizabeth's home. Ten verses, often called Mary's Magnificat because these words magnify the Lord (Luke 1:46-55), erupted from her lips. In her outpouring of praise are at least 15 quotations from the Old Testament. Where did they come from? From scriptures Mary had memorized.

What is coming out of your heart and mouth these days? Obviously, whatever it is, it's something you've been putting there. What you talk about with your workmates, friends, and even family members is an indication of the focus of your heart.

So here's a test. Are you talking truth...or trivia and trash? Are you sharing the Good News...or the latest news? Are you passing on the gospel...or gossip? Proverbs 4:23 advises you to "keep your heart with all diligence, for out of it spring the issues of life." And Jesus cautioned in Matthew 12:34, "Out of the abundance of the heart the mouth speaks."

Why not choose one verse this week to hide in your heart? Maybe even a verse that will enrich your marriage? My favorite for this is Romans 12:10—"Be kindly affectionate to one another with brotherly love, in honor giving preference to one another."

3. *Trust God to guide you through your husband.* Immediately after receiving his first dream from God about Mary, Joseph arose

from sleep and took Mary for his wife. It's interesting to note Mary's silence in response to the adventures that followed. When she was far along in her pregnancy and had to make the long and difficult journey to Bethlehem, she didn't complain. She didn't get upset about having to sleep in a manger or cattle stall. Nor was she negative about packing up in the middle of the night and fleeing to Egypt, or even about returning to live in their hometown of Nazareth.

How many wives do you know who would go through such adventures and not say one negative word? Not one complaint? Imagine the poor husband today who didn't make a reservation in advance, or who took his wife to a hotel or inn where there was no room. Most wives would definitely have a few choice words to say.

But Mary trusted God, and she trusted God to work in her life through her husband. And so should you. Trusting your husband is not always easy, especially if you're not sure he knows where he's going or what he's doing. The solution? Do as God asks of you—love and follow your husband, and pray, pray, pray for God to give your guy wisdom.

4. *Your humility is precious to God.* The angel Gabriel acknowledged Mary with this greeting: "Rejoice, highly favored one, the Lord is with you; blessed are you among women!" (Luke 1:28). Even as a teen, Mary had demonstrated godly character and God acknowledged her worthiness for His privileged assignment of bringing His Son into the world. Her response was one of complete trust and humility as she accepted God's call and His plan for her: "Behold the maidservant of the Lord! Let it be to me according to your word" (Luke 1:38).

There are many in the world who have put Mary on a pedestal to be honored—even worshipped. But the reality of her life would suggest the opposite. Throughout the Gospels and into the early chapters of Acts, Mary is seen as wanting to be no more than a woman after God's own heart, a humble wife and mother, and ultimately a believer in the Christ, her son.

Mary models what the Bible calls "a gentle and quiet spirit." This attitude of humility is described as "very precious in the sight of God" (1 Peter 3:4). Do you want to please God and be precious in His sight? Then put on a heart of humility.

• Lesson for Husbands from Joseph •

We know very little about Joseph. Most of the notoriety in this couple goes to Mary, for obvious reasons. But from what we do know, Joseph was a good and exemplary man who was chosen by God to be the foster-father of God's own Son. In addition to the events we have already considered, we know that Joseph was with Mary when they took Jesus to Jerusalem at age 12 (Luke 2:41-50). The only other reference to Joseph is that he was a carpenter, and the head of a family of at least seven children (Matthew 13:55-56). Even though we are told little about him, we can get a good idea of some of the many qualities he possessed:

1. *Godliness is great gain.* In the first few pages of the biblical record of the birth of Jesus, we see godly men playing key roles.

Zacharias was blameless, a priest, and prophesied concerning the role of his son, John, as the forerunner to Jesus, the Messiah.

Simeon too was described as "just and devout, waiting for the Consolation of Israel, and the Holy Spirit was upon him" (Luke 2:25). He was told by the Holy Spirit that he would see the Messiah before he died. Simeon was rewarded for his faith and held the child Jesus when Mary and Joseph brought Him to be presented in the temple.

Joseph joins this stellar list with God's description of him "being a just man" (Matthew 1:19). In the original Greek text of the New Testament, the word translated "just" is the same one used for Zacharias, which was translated "righteous" in Luke 1:6. God entrusted the safety of Jesus—His very own Son, His beloved Son, His only begotten Son—into Joseph's care during those first few turbulent years after Jesus' birth. Jesus was under Joseph's care until He grew to manhood. Joseph had to be an extraordinary man for God to entrust him with these kinds of responsibilities.

The traits of these godly men, along with the qualifications for church leaders and men of character (found in 1 Timothy 3 and Titus 1), should paint a picture for you of the kind of man God wants you to be. Just as God entrusted His Son to Joseph's care, God has entrusted a precious wife into your care, and perhaps children as well. The job of loving and leading will require that you take advantage of all the tools for maturing spiritually that are offered in God's Word. A strong Christian marriage requires a godly husband and leader.

2. *Listen and learn.* Joseph was sensitive—he listened to the voice of God. God spoke to him through angels, and he listened. Joseph could have easily followed the example of Jonah, a prophet who was given divine instruction to go to Nineveh (Jonah 1:2). And what did Jonah do? He fled in the opposite direction, as far away from God's will as he could go (1:3). Are you thinking, *If God spoke to me through angels, I would make sure to obey Him!* Would you? God has already spoken to you in a much clearer fashion through His Word, the Bible. So how's that working for you? Do you know what He's saying to you? Don't let all your work and responsibilities keep you from reading your Bible. Don't allow your busy schedule to keep you from knowing what God is asking of you.

3. *Obedience is the key to usefulness.* God spoke to Joseph through a dream, and Joseph listened—and obeyed. In every single encounter with God's commands, Joseph immediately, without hesitation,

did as he was instructed. He was like a trained soldier who, in the midst of combat, obeys his commander without question, knowing his obedience is vital to winning the battle.

God is speaking to you and directing you—and your marriage— from His Word. Your obedience to Him will set the tone and pace for your wife and family. Your growth through obedience will draw your wife along in her walk with God. Then together, you can pull your children along with you as they get to know Jesus. But it all starts with your obedience.

4. *Leadership is essential for a husband.* That Joseph was a leader is evident throughout the brief accounts we read about him. Once Joseph understood God's will, he didn't hesitate—he made his decisions and acted on them. Joseph's leadership was based on knowing he was being led by God.

When your decisions are based on your own whims, opinions, and selfish desires, you risk putting your wife in difficult— and maybe even dangerous—positions. But happy is the wife who knows you are receiving your direction from God's Word and wise counsel, who knows you want what's best for her and the family regardless of how much sacrifice is required on your part. When you provide that kind of loving leadership, you make it easier for your wife to fulfill God's calling to lovingly submit. Like Joseph, you have an obligation to lead your marriage and family in the path of God's choosing—not your own.

5. *Selflessness.* This trait is absolutely fundamental. From the moment Joseph heard of Mary's condition, he was thinking of what he could do to save her from gossip and scandal. His selflessness caused him to consider ways he could protect her from embarrassment. "Not wanting to make her a public example, [he] was minded to put her away secretly" (Matthew 1:19).

But God intervened. After hearing God's instructions from the angel, Joseph's selfless decision to wed Mary marked him for the rest of his life. He would share Mary's shame as others began to wonder about her pregnancy. He would probably be seen as the reason for her condition, and his morality would be called into question. His decision to take Mary for his wife would likely expose him to criticism from family, friends, and others in his trade.

Complying with God's will would also involve living on the run, watching his family's backs as others sought to harm God's Son. Little did Joseph know that following God with all his heart would ultimately result in long journeys across some of the most desolate land on earth in order to care for and protect Mary and the child.

Joseph is sending husbands a message that we are to give up our selfish ways. A husband after God's own heart refuses to think of himself. This means the well-being of your wife is your mission and highest priority. "Let nothing be done through selfish ambition or conceit, but in lowliness of mind let each esteem others better than himself. Let each of you look out not only for his own interests, but also for the interests of others" (Philippians 2:3-4).

Try being selfless. Apply these attitudes to your marriage. Your wife will love you for doing so!

Building a Marriage that Lasts

Crises are a fact of life. It's not a matter of *if*, but *when* the next one will hit. This is not morbid introspection; it's just the reality of living in a sinful and chaotic world. So the question you as a couple need to address is this: How are we going to respond to each new crisis as it comes? Roman 8:28 comes to your rescue: "All things work together for good to those who love God, to those who are the called according to His purpose." Knowing that God is in control of all things allows you to trust Him for all things.

Wherever you are in your marriage—whether you are newly-weds or seasoned veterans—resolve together to turn your next crisis over to God as soon as it hits. Believe in God's promise that He will produce good out of that crisis. Refuse to cave in, give up, or run away. Unite your hearts, grasp hold of each other's hands, pray, stand shoulder to shoulder, and face the crisis. Together, do whatever is necessary. And trust God fully, knowing that He is working out His plan for you and your marriage. In the end, you'll be blessed with a stronger marriage because you did it…together.

10

Aquila and Priscilla

Greet Priscilla and Aquila, my fellow workers
in Christ Jesus, who risked their own necks
for my life, to whom not only I give thanks,
but also all the churches of the Gentiles.

ROMANS 16:3-4

Aquila and Priscilla were busy—super busy—working franti-
cally to complete their latest project for the soldiers of the Roman
army. Several legions were bivouacked just outside of Corinth,
where Aquila and Priscilla, professional tentmakers, lived and
worked. The army was designed to be mobile, so most of the time
the men camped in tents. With the size of the military presence
nearby, the two of them were kept busy day and night, stitching
leather strips together to create tents needed by the army.

Today Aquila was especially thankful for his early training. Every
Jewish boy was required to learn a trade, and Aquila's upbringing
had been no exception. His father and grandfather had both been
tentmakers, and it had proved an extremely useful trade.

Aquila and Priscilla had met and married in Rome. As they still had no children, Priscilla was able to work right alongside him, doing her part in the tentmaking business. They liked working together each day, meeting travelers from other places and lands, and hearing their news and tales of adventure.

Ah, Rome! Unfortunately, Aquila and Priscilla's only good memories of Rome were from the past. What a disaster that city was today. Aquila shook his head as he remembered the day he and Priscilla had been forced to leave their home. It all began when Jews who had traveled to Jerusalem for the annual Passover celebration returned home to Rome with an amazing story of salvation through the Messiah, Jesus Christ. Many of the returning Jews had embraced Jesus as their Messiah while they were in Jerusalem. And that's when the trouble started. The Jews who rejected Jesus were angered by the Jews who accepted Jesus. The result? The two factions of Jews in Rome started riots as they battled against one another.

The city officials didn't understand the difference between "Christian Jews" and "Jewish Jews," so, rather than try to sort it out, Emperor Claudius simply evicted all Jews! That's when Aquila and his sweet wife had to join the throngs in an exodus of all Jews from Rome. Because Corinth was such a melting pot of people from different religious backgrounds, they thought it would be the perfect place for the two of them to blend in and quietly settle down.

Yes, those were some tense days—hard days of travel, followed by long days of searching for a place to live, followed by trying days of reestablishing themselves as tentmakers. He and Priscilla still rejoiced every time they remembered their first customer in Corinth.

What's Going On?

In the Bible, we first meet Aquila and Priscilla in Acts 18:2. The year is AD 50. They, along with many other Jews, had been evicted from Rome by Emperor Claudius. Forced to scatter, some of them elected to move to the Greek city of Corinth, including Aquila and Priscilla. There, we find them serving God eagerly and loving others generously.

Starting a Church in Corinth (Acts 18:1-4)

As we step into the story of Aquila and Priscilla, we meet the apostle Paul. He has recently arrived from Athens. Paul's first order of business in Corinth was probably, as was his custom, to find the local synagogue. Once he knew its location, the Jewish quarter would be easy to find. That's when and where God providentially caused Paul to cross paths with Aquila and Priscilla.

> [Paul] found a certain Jew named Aquila, born in Pontus, who had recently come from Italy with his wife Priscilla (because Claudius had commanded all the Jews to depart from Rome); and he came to them. So, because he was of the same trade, he stayed with them and worked; for by occupation they were tentmakers. And he reasoned in the synagogue every Sabbath, and persuaded both Jews and Greeks (18:2-4).

Because Priscilla and Aquila were believers in Christ, it was easy for them to not only work with Paul in their mutual profession, but to minister right alongside Paul as well. They did so for the next year and a half, supporting and helping him while he preached the gospel. The Bible doesn't say, but it's possible this devoted couple began to teach others as well. After all, they were living with a master teacher and evangelist!

Moving to Ephesus (Acts 18:18-19)

Paul stayed 18 months in Corinth. During that time a new church was planted and established. Feeling good about the church's progress, Paul decided to return to his sponsoring church at Antioch, Syria. He could say of his time and ministry in Corinth, "Mission accomplished!"

As an added bonus, Aquila and Priscilla were thrilled when Paul invited them to sail with him and continue to assist him in God's work: "Then [Paul] took leave of the brethren and sailed for Syria, and Priscilla and Aquila were with him...And he came to Ephesus, and left [Priscilla and Aquila] there" (verses 18-19).

Looking at Teamwork (Acts 18:24-28)

While Aquila and Priscilla waited in Ephesus for Paul to return from Antioch, they were actively involved in the local synagogue. One day, a man—a Jew—named Apollos showed up in the synagogue and began to speak boldly:

> Now a certain Jew named Apollos, born at Alexandria, an eloquent man and mighty in the Scriptures, came to Ephesus. This man had been instructed in the way of the Lord; and being fervent in spirit, he spoke and taught accurately the things of the Lord, though he knew only the baptism of John. So he began to speak boldly in the synagogue. When Aquila and Priscilla heard him, they took him aside and explained to him the way of God more accurately (verses 24-26).

Mentoring a Minister (Acts 18:24-28)

When Aquila and Priscilla heard Apollos speak passionately about the things of God, they took him to their home and carefully explained the way of God in greater detail to him. Obviously Aquila and Priscilla had been well taught by Paul. They were quickly able to spot errors in teaching—or in Apollos's case, incomplete information about Jesus. After making the full truth clear to Apollos, they sent him to their friends in Corinth with letters of introduction.

Aquila and Priscilla's friendliness, hospitality, and mentoring had a dramatic impact on the church in Corinth through Apollos: "When he arrived, he greatly helped those who had believed through grace; for he vigorously refuted the Jews publicly, showing from the Scriptures that Jesus is the Christ" (verses 27-28). The church down through the ages benefitted from one faithful couple who was sold out for Jesus and reached out to others.

Using Their Home as a Church in Ephesus (Acts 19)

Another year passed before Paul returned to Ephesus. It was time to plant another church. Paul stayed for two years, and during that time a group of people came from Corinth with a status report on the church there, along with a list of questions. In response to those questions, Paul wrote a letter we know as 1 Corinthians. At the conclusion of this letter he wrote, "The churches of Asia greet you. Aquila and Priscilla greet you heartily in the Lord, with the church that is in their house" (1 Corinthians 16:19). Paul's mention of this couple reveals to us that Aquila and Priscilla's work and ministry in Ephesus had been significant. They had not only opened their hearts to people, but their home as well.

Using Their Home as a Church in Rome

Paul always left his mark wherever he went! In Ephesus, a riot erupted because people were upset at the inroads Christianity had made into the pagan culture in the city (Acts 19:21-41). This riot forced Paul to leave. He chose to return to Corinth, where he then wrote a letter to the churches in Rome (the New Testament book of Romans).

Evidently by this time Priscilla and Aquila had returned to Rome and joined in the work of ministry there. They also hosted a church in their home—near the end of his letter to the Romans, Paul wrote, "Greet Priscilla and Aquila, my fellow workers in Christ Jesus, who risked their own necks for my life, to whom not only

I give thanks, but also all the churches of the Gentiles. Likewise greet the church that is in their house" (Romans 16:3-5).

Serving Where Needed (2 Timothy 4:19)

Fast-forward to the year AD 67, when Paul was in prison in Rome for the second and final time. He busied himself writing and sending the last letter he wrote (2 Timothy) to Timothy, who was pastoring the church in Ephesus. Young Timothy surely needed all the help and encouragement he could get. And guess who was back in Ephesus helping him? Priscilla and Aquila! Paul ended his final letter—and his life—thinking of his old friends, sending them this greeting: "Greet Prisca and Aquila" (verse 19). This dynamic duo had a foundational role in three significant New Testament church ministries—in Rome, Corinth, and Ephesus.

Putting It All Together

Aquila and Priscilla were a phenomenal husband-wife team. They showed us exactly what a couple after God's own heart looks like. They beautifully modeled teamwork and service. The Bible has nothing but positive comments to make about them as individuals and as a couple. Everywhere they went, whether to the nearby Jewish synagogue or helping plant and serve in local churches, people were blessed. Through their examples, this dynamic duo provide many lessons for husbands and wives about love for one another, love for God, and love for His people.

Enjoy this thoughtful summary of their entwined lives:

> Priscilla and Aquila were a couple who accomplished effective ministry behind the scenes. Their tools were hospitality, friendship, and person-to-person teaching. They were not public speakers, but private evangelists. Priscilla and Aquila give us a challenging model of what a couple can do together in the service of Christ. [14]

• Lessons for Husbands and Wives from Aquila and Priscilla •

We can think of Aquila and Priscilla as being like a coin, which has two sides—with each side indicating the same value, but each bearing a different image. Isn't that a perfect picture of what marriage is all about? Like the two sides of a coin, you and your spouse are of the same value, equal in God's eyes. Galatians 3:28 tells us, "There is neither Jew nor Greek, there is neither slave nor free, there is neither male nor female; for you are all one in Christ Jesus." Yet each of you brings something different to your marriage partnership—different personalities. Different spiritual gifts. Different abilities.

We have certainly seen this coin imagery of equality and uniqueness exhibited in Aquila and Priscilla. As individuals they were one of a kind, yet the Bible presents them as a unit. Every time we see their names, they are together. Sometimes their names are given in a different order, and we also see Priscilla's nickname Prisca used. But we never find them mentioned individually. So what can you learn from this "power couple" who chose to serve actively wherever they went?

1. *Work as a team.* Aquila and Priscilla worked together to host churches in their homes. They also worked as a team when they talked to and enlightened the great preacher, Apollos, giving him more accurate information about Jesus. The implications are obvious. Working as a team can produce a highly effective ministry. Because two are involved, more can be accomplished. And, as the wise King Solomon pointed out in Ecclesiastes, "Two are better than one" (4:9).

When it comes to service and the use of your spiritual gifts, both of you are responsible for the development and use of your own spiritual gifts. But it's possible you will have times when, like

Priscilla and Aquila, you and your spouse can work together in mutual ministry. Plan for them. Prepare for them. And proceed when the opportunities come your way. Like Priscilla and Aquila, as a team, you will be a stronger force than either one of you individually.

And here's an added plus: Working as a team doesn't mean you are both always doing exactly the same thing at the same time. Maybe one of you is serving in the kitchen while the other is setting up chairs, or teaching the Bible study, or overseeing childcare. Many times, when one of us is teaching at a conference, the other is standing at the book table and talking with people. Or while Jim is off in some wilderness with a group of men or missionaries, I hold down the fort at home.

Sometimes you'll work together—hosting, greeting, serving in a food line, attending a meeting, cleaning up in the kitchen. And other times you'll divide and conquer, each setting out in a different direction, always looking forward to reuniting at the end of the day to share God's blessings and hear about how He used each of you.

2. *Grow together in the faith.* You might say Aquila and Priscilla were "homeschooled" in their knowledge and understanding of God. They were fortunate to have the writer of 13 books of the New Testament living right under their very own roof. And blessing upon blessing, they also worked side by side with Paul every day in Corinth. Can you imagine the lively discussions they had each day, the question-and-answer sessions they had as they sat together sewing strips of leather to make tents? After many months of this kind of daily training, along with any learning Aquila and Priscilla were doing on their own, they must have developed a strong understanding of the Messiah, His mission on earth, and the gospel of salvation. After all, look at who their teacher was!

Then Paul, their mentor, dropped the dynamic duo off in Ephesus. Now Aquila and Priscilla were ready to open their home to others and to discuss and teach the truths of the gospel themselves. So when Apollos came to Ephesus and started preaching in the synagogue, Priscilla and Aquila were ready to do a bit of tutoring: "So [Apollos] began to speak boldly in the synagogue. When Aquila and Priscilla heard him, they took him aside and explained to him the way of God more accurately" (Acts 18:26). They both shared in the teaching.

Being mentored is vital for spiritual growth. Do you and your spouse each have a mentor? Someone you meet with regularly? Someone who can point you to books, classes, and seminars that will help you grow in your faith? Someone who's willing to answer your questions—even the sticky ones? Someone who will guide you through the seasons and phases of your marriage, your career, raising your children? No price can be put on the wisdom and instruction you receive from a good Christian mentor.

In a perfect world, the two of you, as a couple, would be equal in your spiritual maturity. But in reality, the best you can aim for is that you are both growing in the Lord. Commit to encouraging each other every day at whatever pace each is able to keep. Keep your eyes on the goal—every day is a day you should both be growing stronger in faith.

3. *Open your home to others.* Aquila and Priscilla did something that any couple can do: They opened up their home for guests, meetings, and church services. This was how the early church grew. There were no church buildings. Therefore, evangelism and edification occurred as believers welcomed others into their homes for outreach and worship. The Bible never says that Priscilla and Aquila did the teaching at these house meetings, even though they were thoroughly capable, given the training they received from Paul. All we are told is that they opened their home so Christians could gather together for church.

You could open your home for ministry purposes, couldn't you?

It may take a little effort to tidy the house and have a few refreshments available for a church or study group, but this is almost a no-brainer opportunity. Just make your home available, swing open the front door, and say, "Hey, welcome! Come on in. Make yourselves at home!" As you do this, you will set a positive example for other couples who are looking for a way to minister together.

And a big bonus? You'll be doing as you are exhorted in God's Word: "Be hospitable to one another without grumbling" (1 Peter 4:9). And "Do not forget to entertain strangers" (Hebrews 13:2).

Building a Marriage that Lasts

The remarkable husband-wife team, Aquila and Priscilla, provide a perfect portrait of mutual love centered on God and each other. What a way to close this part of this book! They give us a divine glimpse of how a marriage can and should function. We can be sure their marriage was not without its share of struggles and setbacks. In fact, they may have experienced difficulties that forced them to fall back on God and lean on each other. Maybe it was the hard times that contributed to making theirs a marriage that lasted.

Aquila and Priscilla and the other couples we have surveyed through this book each possessed their own unique strengths and weaknesses. Like them, you and your teammate bring a different set of abilities and a singular personality into your marriage. You will spend the rest of your lives working together (and don't miss the operative word—*together*) to live out God's will for you as a husband and as a wife. With His help, you will become in reality what you already are physically: one flesh, one person in your thinking and your actions.

How will this be accomplished? The apostle Paul, the great inspired marriage counselor, advises that you and your spouse be

> of the same mind, maintaining the same love, united in spirit, intent on one purpose. Do nothing from selfishness or empty conceit, but with humility of mind regard one another as more important than yourselves; do not merely look out for your own personal interests, but also for the interests of others. Have this attitude in yourselves which was also in Christ Jesus (Philippians 2:2-5 NASB).

PART TWO

Thirty Days of
Growing Together

Before You Begin

Hi there! And welcome to this special section created just for you as a couple after God's own heart. In this part of your book, we have prepared devotions that focus on God, His character, and His promises. We've always appreciated any help others could give us as we seek to grow as a couple and as Christians, and we wanted to include this section to help you on your way to greater spiritual growth...and to a greater marriage. These short devotional readings come to you with our prayers that you will rejoice as you grow closer to each other because you are each growing closer to God.

Whenever we speak—whether individually, or as a couple at a marriage conference, or on a radio program with call-in questions—it almost never fails that we are asked something like, "How can I get my husband (or wife) to have devotions together with me?" A Christian husband or wife who is seeking to place God first in their marriage wants to experience spiritual growth together with their partner in marriage.

Maybe to some, the idea of couples having devotions together is merely a myth. But it doesn't have to be that way—those who have tried it have found it to be a good idea. No, they've found it a *great* idea! Surely God loves to see His couples seek truth, strength, and guidance from His Word and seal their discoveries with a prayer...together!

Believe us when we say we know that carving out even a small amount of time each day for anything is a gigantic challenge. But time together in God's Word and a few moments in prayer will make a difference in your marriage, in your family, and in your day.

To start having a daily together-time that's centered on God, try a few of these proven tips.

- Set a time. Talk it over, agree on it, and give it a try. If necessary, you can adjust the time later, but the most important thing is getting started.

- Mix it up. Maybe you'll want to each read the devotion for the day separately and then come together to discuss it and pray. Or you may try taking turns reading the daily devotions out loud, or trade off reading every other paragraph. There's no right or wrong way to have couple devotions. Just do it, and...

- Enjoy being together. Even if you are already together a lot, there is nothing like being together with a spiritual focus. Having couple devotions is not supposed to feel like taking medicine. No, it should be like going out together on a dessert date. You'll often find that the handful of minutes you spend communicating with the Lord and each other will turn out to be the best minutes of your day.

- Praise God together. When it comes to growing in the Lord, our favorite couple verse is Psalm 34:3. We are praying this scripture for you and asking God to richly bless the two of you.

Oh, magnify the LORD with me,
and let us exalt His name together.

The Promise

What is a promise? The dictionary defines the word *promise* as "a statement, either oral or written, assuring that one will or will not do something." It's a vow, or a pledge.

You've probably made a few vows and pledges in your lifetime—to your spouse when you exchanged wedding vows and pledged your undying love, to your local church as a member, to a company's code of ethics, to a branch of the government, to the armed forces, or even to a close friend. So you have some experience with promises, vows, and pledges.

In the next 30 days you will look at the promises of God… and God's power to follow through and keep His promises. This is important because *the power of a promise depends on the one making the promise.*

And, dear reading couple, that means you can trust in God's promises. Why? Because of God's nature and character. God is described as the "God, who cannot not lie" (Titus 1:2). Therefore, you can be confident that if there is a promise in God's Word that has an application for you, you can accept that promise with full assurance. God will do His part to fulfill that promise. It's His nature. And God cannot lie!

Are you willing...to put God's promises to work in your life? The Bible offers many powerful promises. God's promises are there for the taking. God would not offer what He is unable or unwilling to give. So you can be assured of the legitimacy of His promises. When it comes to putting God's powerful promises to work in your life and marriage, the issue will never be with God. No, it will always be with you and your willingness to do your part to put God's power and promises to work.

Are you willing...to do what God asks of you? Tapping into the power of God's promises will demand something from and of you. "What will be required of me?" you ask. A firm resolve to do what God asks.

And before either of you throw your hands up in defeat, realize that God is not asking for perfection. No, God knows us well, and He knows our weaknesses. He is only asking for progression—progression indicated by...

- a willingness to follow God even though at times you stumble and fall (Philippians 3:14),
- a willingness to ask for forgiveness when you falter (1 John 1:9), and
- a willingness to stay in the battle (and it is a battle!) of becoming a couple after God's own heart (Acts 13:22).

The truth is, the promises are yours. Are you ready and willing to put them to work in your life? In your marriage? If so, read on to discover God's powerful promises...for you! The next 30 days will be an immeasurable blessing in your relationship and journey together!

Father, may we grow to trust your promises more and more and reap the blessings You desire to give us.

The Couple Who Prays Together

Where do you live? We happen to live in a house that sits on a hill. That means our home was built with several levels. Each day one of us writes on one level in the house and the other writes on another. To communicate with each other from office to office while we're working on our manuscripts, we use walkie-talkies.

One day recently when our grandchildren were with us, they spotted the walkie-talkies and, of course, they wanted to talk on them. After explaining how they worked, we gave one to Jacob and one to Katie.

Well, it wasn't long before both children came back, pagers in hand, crying and complaining that the walkie-talkies were broken. Because they were too young to understand how to send and receive messages, Jacob and Katie were sure the problem was with the walkie-talkies.

We are probably all a lot like our grandchildren: We don't understand how to communicate with God! Then, when we think our prayers aren't being answered, we tend to get discouraged and blame God. We think God is the problem. We question, "Why isn't God answering my prayers?" But as you look at God's promise of answered prayer, you'll see that God always comes through. Hear Jesus Himself offer this promise:

> Ask, and it will be given to you; seek, and you will
> find; knock, and it will be opened to you. For every-
> one who asks receives, and he who seeks finds, and to
> him who knocks it will be opened (Matthew 7:7-8).

God does answer your prayers! In fact, He promises to answer you when you pray. And sometimes He answers when you don't even know how to pray about a certain issue. When that happens, the Holy Spirit steps in and "intercedes for us" (Romans 8:26 NASB). But usually you know what your needs are—as individuals and as a couple—and who or what you should be praying for. So God asks you to *ask*.

Discuss the possibility of praying together. If the two of you agree to give it a try, or to reinstitute praying as a couple, be content to start out slowly. The two of you can begin by praying a sentence each when you say grace with your meal or when you lean against one another while giving your good-bye hugs in the morning.

Honestly, our favorite prayer time together is when we get into bed in the evening, turn the lights out, hold hands, and pray briefly for people, friends, family, and those who asked us to pray for them.

Don't miss out on this opportunity to strengthen your marriage. Make it a point—and a practice—to come before the Lord in prayer together as a couple. It doesn't have to be elaborate, or formal, or take more than a few minutes. Make it as simple and easy and natural as you can for both of you.

And the result? You will both be blessed. And it will also do wonders for your marriage. After all, what is the old saying? "The couple who prays together *stays* together." Prayer together is a shared spiritual experience. It is a strong tie that binds two hearts and souls together. And imagine the mutual joy you'll experience as you witness God's answers to your prayers…together!

Lord, You promise to hear our prayers. May our hearts desire to commune with You daily!

Adapt and Transform

Jim is a former member in the medical field, which means he still reads medical journals and clips articles that catch his eye. One such article was a report on a study that was conducted on several thousand men and women who had lived beyond their life expectancy. Many of the people in the study were well into their nineties, and some were more than a hundred years old. In assessing the secrets to longevity, the researchers looked at personality, dietary habits, physical exercise, and the abuse of substances such as alcohol and tobacco.

While reading along, Jim (as you probably would, too) immediately assumed that the longevity factor had to be attributed to what these people ate or drank. He surmised, "They must have eaten tofu and seaweed and drank gallons of purified water from some guarded mountain stream!"

But, surprise, surprise, the researchers reported that the common denominator was not what these people did or did not consume. No, most of these very, very senior citizens had placed few restrictions on their physical habits.

Do you know what the common thread was that ran through the lives of all these "survivors"? In one word, it was *adaptability*.

These people apparently lived longer because they had an ability to change—change with the seasons of their lives, change with the deaths of spouses, change with their surroundings.

How do you rate in the Change Department? Like it or not, we are all part of a changing world. Jobs come and go. The size of the family keeps expanding...and contracting. Relationships and health are uncertain. Life has its changing seasons. And with each one, you as a couple must adapt.

Change is not limited to the physical, marital, and vocational realms. In fact, change is more critical in the spiritual realm than in all the others. Why? Because we serve a God whose specialty is change and transformation.

Ever since the fall of Adam and Eve in the Garden of Eden, God has desired to call the lost back to Him and create a race of spiritually redeemed people—a people who would love Him, follow Him, and obey Him. God's plan for bringing this about came to a climax with the incarnation of Jesus Christ. It's because of Christ's life, death, and resurrection that salvation is possible. When we come into a relationship with Christ, God promises—*promises*— to bring about a radical change in our lives! How radical? God is committed to nothing less than an entirely new order of creation. This is how His powerful promise reads:

> If anyone is in Christ, he is a new creation; old things have passed away; behold, all things have become new (2 Corinthians 5:17).

God is not interested in preserving the status quo. In the Old Testament, He promised to give His people "a new heart" and put "a new spirit" in them, to take away their "heart of stone" and replace it with "a heart of flesh" (Ezekiel 36:26).

Change can be either good or bad. When change occurs, you are either growing in faith and knowledge...or you are slipping back into old ways, old habits, old actions, and old attitudes. You simply cannot rest on past change! *Today* is a new day with new challenges for you as individuals and as a couple. You must ask God *today* for His enabling power to further conform you to the image of His Son.

Then *tomorrow* you must get up (again) and ask God (again) for power (again) for one more day of change. Do whatever you must to ensure that the old ways don't creep back into your life and cause you to slip into your former sinful patterns. The battle for godly change is constant. And, let's face it, it will be ongoing until we meet our Savior face-to-face. The Holy Spirit has invaded your heart, soul, and body—and marriage!—with new life, and nothing is the same.

Father, may we look to every challenge as an opportunity to grow closer to You and more like Your Son.

Forget and Forget… and Forget!

Although I've never attended one of my high school reunions, I've heard about them! My friends have told me about classmates who still look the way they always did and about others whose personalities haven't changed at all. They also report that others are larger—or balder!—and almost unrecognizable. Also, and sadly, some who enjoyed success during their high school years have gone the way of alcoholism, suffered disabilities, and encountered other tragedies.

The past. It makes us who we are. It teaches us lessons about God, about life, and about ourselves. We learn volumes from what lies behind. But our learning must not stop there. We must then take those lessons and move ahead. This is exactly the truth the apostle Paul teaches:

> Forgetting what is behind and straining toward what is ahead, I press on toward the goal to win the prize for which God has called me heavenward in Christ Jesus (Philippians 3:13-14 NIV).

Forgetting what lies behind is not always easy. Your marriage may be plagued by memories of past sin, hurtful words, betrayals, or times when you've been let down. Note what Paul says in the verses above—the word "forgetting" is in the *present* tense. You see, forgetting is not an act done once and for all. Instead, like Paul, we must *keep on forgetting* those things in the past that hold us back. Paul didn't want to rest on his past accomplishments, and neither should we. And Paul didn't want his past mistakes to keep him from moving on, and neither should we.

The past is over. It is no longer real. So don't dwell on it. And don't let it hold you back. Forget whatever would keep you and your spouse from moving forward in faith and in your spiritual growth. Look at the past only to remember God's role in the problems and pain of yesterday—to recall His presence, His faithfulness, His compassion, and His gracious provision in times of trial.

God's love for you accomplished the forgiveness of your sin, your cleansing, your new birth, and your fresh start. Sure, consequences of your actions may remain, but the sin itself is forgiven. You are covered and cleansed by Christ's precious blood. You can, therefore, go on with your life…without shame and without being held back. And you can show your love for God by refusing to dwell on what He has removed and taken care of. When your past sin comes to mind, acknowledge God's forgiveness, thank Him profusely, and move on with praise and thanksgiving.

Lord, You have forgiven us and made us new in Christ. May we rejoice in Your provision and faithfulness!

The God of All Comfort

When people think of comfort, they usually think immediately of the female partner in the marriage. A wife lovingly nurtures her husband, her children, her friends, a stray cat, and you name it—it's her nature! And through all of the times of heartache and pain, she is right there to offer comfort to all.

But are we correct to attribute comfort only to the female side of the human species? Is a guy's manhood resistant to the idea that he, too, should have a compassionate side?

If you desire to become more "Godlike" and "Christlike" in your actions and attitudes, then look at this next assurance from God. In it, we discover a powerful promise that is intimate, tender, and heartwarming. It is a picture of God, the Father, consoling His own.

> Blessed be the God and Father of our Lord Jesus Christ, the Father of mercies and God of all comfort, who comforts us in all our tribulation (2 Corinthians 1:3-4).

To many Christians, this promise is the most compelling passage on comfort found in the New Testament. The apostle Paul speaks repeatedly about the concept of comfort (2 Corinthians 1:1-7). And he speaks specifically of God's promise of comfort for those of His children who are experiencing suffering and hardship.

God is "the Father of mercies." It's a part of His nature. Scripture describes God as a father who has "compassion" for His children and whose "lovingkindness…is from everlasting to everlasting" (Psalm 103:13,17 NASB). So we can see that compassion is a constant and significant part of God's nature.

Paul also adds that God is "the God of all comfort." He is always ready to comfort you. Whatever your hardship—big or small—it doesn't matter, for the God of *all* comfort is available to help you. Are you hurting physically or emotionally? Are things not going well at work? At home? Is there some temptation you're struggling with, or an area in which you need support? Do you need encouragement? In all of these and more, believe it—God is there to help and to comfort.

And what are you to do with the comfort God gives? Enjoy it, to be sure! Let it teach you, most definitely! Be faithful to pass it on to others who are suffering, beginning at home. Every trial you endure, through God's grace, helps you comfort others—and especially your spouse—when they are suffering hardships. God's blessed comfort is not only to cheer *you* up, but it is also intended to cheer *others* too.

Learn to share the comfort you've received from God. Don't shy away from this important ministry to others. Instead, develop a heart of compassion (Colossians 3:12). Jesus is the perfect example. He constantly demonstrated compassion as He walked this earth, comforting any and all. Make the Master your model.

Lord, thank You for all the comfort You have shown us, even when we don't recognize it. And may we gladly share that comfort with others.

Unfinished Work

Are you a person who loves to start projects, practices, and ministries? As a couple, we've fit this description for about 35 years of marriage. And it's been a great joy to see many of our ventures come to pass and continue on.

But here's a confession—we can also tend to not finish some of our projects (and we have a storage unit to prove it!). Beginning a new undertaking is thrilling, especially when you're visionaries and have lots of ideas. But, oh boy, as we carry out that venture, is it ever easy to get distracted by yet another new dream…and then, before we know it, we're off and running like a dog with a juicy new bone with that latest inspiration!

That's when we realize how fortunate we are to have other dear souls who come alongside us to help finish what we've started. On the top of our "thanksgiving" list to God are the names of many wonderful friends and committed finishers. But most of all, we— and you—can thank God that when it comes to our eternal destiny, *He* is both a starter *and* a finisher.

Do you ever feel that you as a couple are not making much progress in your spiritual life? That you take two steps forward in your growth…only to fall back one (or is it two)? Are you becoming discouraged by shortcomings and slow growth in either of you? Do you feel unfinished? Incomplete?

Well, take heart. When God starts a project (that's you!), He completes it. God has promised that He will help all who embrace His Son as Savior to grow in His grace until He has completed— yes, *completed*—His work in our lives.

That's what this present promise is all about. When the apostle Paul wrote his letter to the believers in the Philippian church, he expressed excitement because he had heard that his beloved friends were maturing in their Christian faith. And as he wrote to his comrades-in-Christ, Paul shared his confidence that God would be faithful to continue the spiritual growth process in their lives.

And friends, God will continue that process until it is completed in you as well. That's a promise! Read it for yourself. Read Paul's powerful, encouraging, and comforting words of confidence to his friends...and to you!

> For I am confident of this very thing, that He who
> began a good work in you will perfect it until the day
> of Christ Jesus (Philippians 1:6 NASB).

What a faithful God You are! When we feel as though we're falling short, may we rest assured that You will carry on Your work in us to completion.

"Seek Ye First"

If you're like us, you want your children to have some of the things you didn't have when you were growing up. And you certainly don't want them to make the same mistakes you did. Put another way, you want them to have a better life, to *live* a better life. In short, you're ambitious or desirous of their success. But beware! Such ambition could backfire. Sadly, Rebekah, the wife of Isaac, is an illustration of this reality.

Are you worried about the social and financial status of your children? Many moms worry about their children going to the "best" schools, living in the "best" neighborhood, meeting the "right" people for the connections needed to get ahead. This is basically what Rebekah did. She manipulated her favored son, her husband, and her less-favored son in order to advance her ambitious desires for her son Jacob's "best"—for his position, wealth, and welfare.

And what was the result? Jacob had to literally run for his life. He was forced to flee from his home in order to avoid the murderous wrath of his brother. Sadly, Rebekah never saw her precious Jacob again.

What do you imagine the family situation would have been

like in the face of a lifetime of such partiality and deception, and after something as drastic as one son seeking to murder the other, causing a family split? If it was bad before such a rift, it could only have been worse afterward. Most likely, it was unbearable.

Rebekah's aspirations for her son moved her to take matters into her own hands and created a family disaster. Dreaming about bettering your children's lives is not a bad thing. You should want to make sure your children are properly educated and develop self-discipline and self-motivation. You should want your children to succeed and contribute positively to society and their future families. But you should never desire these things at the expense of godly principles.

Focus *your* attention on living for God and trusting in His care. Then train your children in righteousness. Show them the way—and the why—of making choices that please God. Then pray faithfully and trust the Lord to lead them and give them direction for their future careers, jobs, and marriage partners. In the words of Jesus,

> Seek first his kingdom and his righteousness, and all these things will be given to you as well (Matthew 6:33 NIV).

Lord, remind us daily that when we put You first, You will take care of everything else.

The Playbook

I once heard of a good football team that was defeated by a weaker team. It didn't matter what play was run—the opponent seemed to know exactly how to defend against the play. The coaches on the stronger team were mystified as they tried to make sense of their loss. Then, sometime later, the mystery was solved: One of their playbooks had gotten into the hands of the opposing team. The stolen playbook gave the opposing team a guide to victory. They knew every play the other team might possibly attempt.

God has given us, as Christians, a playbook as well—the Bible. This means we can make a successful defense against the "flaming arrows of the evil one" (Ephesians 6:16 NASB). So purpose together as a couple to follow God's advice—always.

> Only be strong and very courageous; be careful to do according to all the law which Moses My servant commanded you; do not turn from it to the right or to the left, so that you may have success wherever you go (Joshua 1:7 NASB).

As a team, don't get distracted and lose your courage. Don't turn to the right or to the left. Keep your devotion focused on God and His playbook for you and your marriage "so that you may have success wherever you go" (Joshua 1:7 NASB).

When Joshua was getting ready to go into battle, he had every reason to be afraid. First, he was following in the sandals of the bigger-than-life Moses, the same Moses who talked to God and who had led the people out of Egypt. Then there was his army... if you could call it that! His men were a ragtag band with little or no military training and experience in battle. And finally, there was the enemy. Joshua had seen them himself. They were giants, of savage tribes who refused to give up their land without a fierce fight (Numbers 13:32; 14:45).

Knowing all of this, God said to Joshua, "Be strong and courageous." He was like a coach on the sidelines, encouraging Joshua to "lead these people to victory—give them the land!"

Joshua could go into battle with courage, knowing that God had promised victory. God was not going to allow him to fail.

God's reassurance of His promise to Joshua should give every Christian couple confidence. God has promised you the victory. Do you believe that? Then trust Him. "Thanks be to God who always leads us in triumph in Christ" (2 Corinthians 2:14). That's a promise! You can have full confidence in the battles you face and fight in life. Pray to face them with God's promised courage.

God, we know Your promises will never fail. May we get to know Your promises, engrave them upon our hearts, and let them be our source of confidence and hope in every situation we encounter.

The Way Out

Living for 30 years in Southern California with the constant threat of earthquakes has made our family a bit cautious whenever we go into buildings. And this wariness was especially acute right after the 6.8-magnitude killer earthquake in Northridge, California—the epicenter of which was only three miles from our home. Even today, years after that quake, as we enter a building, we immediately look for the exit signs. We instinctively wonder, *Where are they?* And, *What is the quickest way to get to them?* We aren't paranoid (or are we?). We must still be looking for the "big one"!

Now, you may never have to contend with earthquakes, but what about your last plane trip? What was the first thing the flight attendants told you? They instructed you on how to exit the plane during an emergency, didn't they? Exit routes are very important to know, whether for fire safety, plane mishaps, earthquake survival... or even when dealing with temptation.

Temptation comes into every believer's life. Not one of us is immune (and you know what we're talking about!). So how would you like a promise for victory over temptation? Great news—God has a promise for you!

No temptation has overtaken you but such as
is common to man; and God is faithful, who will
not allow you to be tempted beyond what you are
able, but with the temptation will provide the way
of escape also, so that you will be able to endure it
(1 Corinthians 10:13 NASB).

In these reassuring words, God promises you and us deliverance from sin. In other words, this is God's promise of an "exit." God isn't showing us *how* to exit our dangerous situations. No, He is showing us how *He* will provide an exit so we won't succumb to life's temptations.

So you should not view temptation as a bad thing. It is neither bad nor good. It is simply an opportunity for you to reaffirm and strengthen your faith and trust in God.

And here's another important fact: Temptation should not be viewed as sin. Rather, *giving in* to a temptation is sin.

Temptation, when resisted, can help build your spiritual muscles much like the iron weights in the gym build up physical muscles. The more you can hold out against temptation, the stronger your spiritual muscles become. So it's vital for you to resist temptation as much as you can.

But what if the temptation gets too heavy for you to bear? This is where God's promise of deliverance comes to your rescue and saves the day. He's not a spectator in your lives. He's actively involved and ever present. He wants to help. And when temptations become too heavy to handle on your own, He delivers you by providing an escape route, an exit out of the temptation. The way out.

Father, You are so good to enable us with Your strength in our time of need. With You at our side, we have nothing to fear.

Once and for All

~

Christmas is a festive and joyous time of the year. And, as your joint checking account will testify, gift-giving is a prominent element of the holiday season!

If you're like us, you probably received a few gifts that you aren't sure what to do with—gifts that don't fit or you don't need. They were given by well-meaning friends and family, but you probably saved the original boxes so you could return them as soon as possible!

What about those "perfect" gifts that were ideal for you and even useful? You wore that shirt or that robe until it became a rag. And you're still using that power tool or food mixer.

God has given the two of you an even more cherished and useful gift—a life-saving one! He gave the gift of His Son, the Lord Jesus Christ. The apostle Paul called God's gift of Jesus "His indescribable gift" (2 Corinthians 9:15).

When you receive God's gift of Jesus, you also receive the promise of God's forgiveness. And note how complete this forgiveness is:

> As far as the east is from the west, so far has He removed our transgressions from us (Psalm 103:12).

Are you struggling with any sin you think is too big for God to forgive? Remember that God is bigger than all your sin. Sure, there may be an aftermath you will have to deal with in your life. Broken relationships are hard to mend, broken laws have their just penalties, borrowed and mismanaged money must be repaid. But God's cleansing love and forgiveness will see you through any and all consequences.

How about the other end of the sin-spectrum? Maybe you think your sin is too small for God to care about or notice—you know, those "little white lies," those careless acts of indiscretion. You may be wishfully thinking these little sins are so small that they are "undetectable" on God's radar screen.

But these unconfessed sins do have a consequence. They hinder your fellowship with a holy and just God. (And guess what? They hinder your fellowship with your spouse!) It's true that God forgives sin, but it's also true He overlooks none. So whether your sins are big or small, you need to experience God's promise of forgiveness for them.

When you receive Jesus Christ, your sins are forgiven once and for all. When Jesus uttered, "It is finished" on the cross, He was speaking of His work of redemption (John 19:30). Every sin that you will ever commit is covered by Jesus' death.

God's forgiveness is complete because Jesus' work is complete. God's justice was satisfied when His Son died. God can therefore show His mercy and complete forgiveness to you.

Lord, may we never take Your forgiveness for granted, and may we never fail to remember what it cost You to make that forgiveness possible.

Without Ceasing

Elizabeth here! When I was a junior in high school, I played the violin. I didn't exactly excel at it, even with practice. But for sure, you didn't want to hear me when I didn't practice! Prayer is like that. Prayer, like anything else done faithfully and regularly, in time becomes more natural and normal. But when we are irregular at prayer, we feel awkward and don't quite know what to say to God. God doesn't expect you to wait until you can word your prayers flawlessly. He just wants to hear from you. As a couple, make the changes necessary to form the habit of checking in with God on a regular basis—preferably daily!

That's what David, "the sweet psalmist of Israel" (2 Samuel 23:1), did. He declared to God,

> In the morning, LORD, you hear my voice; in the morning I lay my requests before you and wait expectantly (Psalm 5:3 NIV).

Another psalmist exulted, "*Seven times a day* I praise You" (Psalm 119:164), indicating that he prayed and praised numerous times because of a continual attitude of praise. When you fail to pray, you are in a sense saying you don't need God. And here's another thought—when you fail to pray, you are also saying that you're probably not even thinking about God! How can I say that? Because any and every thought about God moves our hearts to pray.

If we can give you one piece of advice, it's this: Pray faithfully. Faithfulness is a mark of maturity. Faithful people can be trusted in what they say and do. And faithfulness is a necessary element in any relationship, especially a relationship with God. We know God is faithful. He is unchanging and unchangeable. Faithfulness is one of His attributes. So to keep up your part of a relationship with God, you need to be faithful to God. And the best way to be faithful as a couple is through a committed and constant prayer life.

The breathing in of air sustains life. It's a basic fact—as long as you breathe, you live. Therefore no sane person would ever decide, "I think I'll take some time off from breathing." No, breathing is necessary for life. And you must see prayer in the same way. Prayer is necessary for the Christian life, as well as for a better life. Just as you will breathe for as long as you live, you must also pray for as long as you live. Do it for life!

Lord, You are so faithful to us. May we be faithful to You—with prayers that seek You at all times, in all places, for all things.

Undeserved

~

Grace. Just say the word, and many think immediately of the Christian hymn "Amazing Grace." And, truly, the story of the writer of this hymn is all about the amazing grace of God.

John Newton was a slave trader who plied his business in the 1800s. He was a rough and immoral man who later described himself as a "wretch"—which, from all accounts, he was…and more! Through a set of severe, life-threatening circumstances, Newton experienced a dramatic conversion that changed his heart and his way of life. He went on to become a famous preacher and songwriter. No wonder the first line of his hymn marvels, "Amazing grace, how sweet the sound that saved a wretch like me!"

Yes, God's grace is amazing. What's more, God says this:

My grace is sufficient for you (2 Corinthians 12:9).

Have you ever done something bad—*really* bad? You knew you were wrong, and so did everyone else. And yet, your spouse, or your boss, or your children forgave you? Then you've tasted a little of what it means to receive mercy that was not warranted. That's what God's grace is! Simply put, "grace" is God's mercy, God's favor—God's *unmerited* favor.

From the very beginning of recorded history, God has demonstrated His favor, starting with Adam and Eve. This couple willfully disobeyed God and deserved the punishment of death for their disobedience. But God showed forth His grace—His favor—toward them instead, which was definitely unmerited!

And so it has been down through Bible history. The nation of Israel is another example of God's grace. The people deserved destruction, but God was gracious and did not abandon them.

Now let's fast-forward to today, to you. The Bible clearly states that "all [and that "all" means all!] have sinned and fall short of the glory of God" (Romans 3:23), and that "the wages of sin is death" (Romans 6:23). Like all those who have gone before you, you don't deserve God's favor, either. You deserve death. But (and here comes God's undeserved favor), "by grace you have been saved through faith, and that not of yourselves; it is the gift of God" (Ephesians 2:8).

Grace is God's intentional bestowal of His loving favor on those whom He saves. You can't earn grace. If you could, it would no longer be unmerited. And you cannot save yourselves. Only God can save you. The only way for you to receive this gift of God's grace is by faith in Jesus Christ (Romans 3:24).

Friends, has God's grace been poured out on you through Jesus Christ? If so, then you have experienced God's amazing, sufficient, and undeserved grace.

Lord, thank You for Your abounding grace in our lives. May our gratitude abound as well!

Running in Circles

Over the years I (Jim) have made a serious commitment to keep in shape by jogging. On occasion, this decision has presented its own set of unique problems. For instance, the time I was jogging in Paris, France. While I was there visiting a missionary friend and his family, I decided to get up early before our meetings began and go for a run. It was a glorious spring day, the kind Paris is famous for. So off I went.

As I ran, I sort of paid attention to my surroundings. But then, as I usually do when I'm running, I got lost in my thoughts. I always run for a specific number of minutes, so that morning, when half of my allotted time was up, I turned around to head back to my friend's apartment building. But to my surprise, when I did my about-face, nothing looked familiar! It was still very early in the morning, so only a few people were out. And the street signs and storefronts were in French...of which I did not know even one word to use in asking for help. Basically, I was lost in Paris!

That's when I told myself that if I ran around for a while, eventually I would see a familiar sight and would then know how to make my way back. But after running around in circles for some time, nothing was looking even remotely familiar! It was then I began to get nervous. Why hadn't I thought to bring my friend's address, or at least his phone number? I had even left my passport at the apartment. And if I didn't get out of this mess soon, I could see myself lost forever on the streets of Paris!

Friends, when all else fails, pray. Now, isn't that usually the way it goes? I didn't think of praying until I was about ready to push the panic button. "Lord," I asked, "please show me something that will help guide me back to the apartment."

Was it "coincidence," or answered prayer? (I think you know the answer!) Almost before I could finish my cry to God, I saw it—the Talbot truck showroom sign. Why had the sign made such an impression? It's because *Talbot* is the name of the seminary where I received my theological training. And for that reason I had made a special note of the truck showroom when I passed by it. Within ten minutes, I was safely back at the apartment.

Have you ever had a similar experience? Were you lost and in need of directions? Or were you in the midst of serious decision-making as a couple and needed guidance? Well, God has a promise just for you!

> Trust in the LORD with all your heart and do not lean on your own understanding. In all your ways acknowledge Him, and He will make your paths straight (Proverbs 3:5-6 NASB).

Take note: In this promise from God, He does not guarantee that any one of us won't get lost in a foreign city. But He does promise to give you a lifetime of guidance...if you want it.

Lord, You promise guidance when we need it. May we always bring our needs to You right away!

Grounded in Hope

We are hoping and praying that this is not true about you, but sadly, most people don't know what they are reaching for in life. They don't know their purpose. So what do they do? They fixate on wealth, power, relationships, and health. They believe that achievement in these spheres will satisfy their inner longings.

But do such conquests really accomplish that? Are couples truly happy when they achieve fitness, finances, influence, and friendships?

The answer is *yes* to some extent. But friends, there is more—so much more—to life! As one miserable man wrote in his suicide note, "I am worth ten million dollars as men judge things, but I am so poor in spirit that I cannot live any longer. Something is terribly wrong with life."

What, we wonder, was missing from this man's life?

In a word...*hope!* Have you heard this saying? "You can live 40 days without food, five minutes without air, but you can't live even one second without hope." Real hope, a confident hope, is what people—even that wealthy, successful businessman—are longing for. But they make the mistake of looking for it in all the wrong places.

True and lasting hope is revealed in only one place—the Bible.

True and lasting hope is found in only one person—Jesus Christ. And true and lasting hope is promised from only one source—God! Hear now one of His many powerful promises of hope:

> "For I know the plans I have for you," declares the LORD, "plans to prosper you and not to harm you, plans to give you hope and a future" (Jeremiah 29:11 NIV).

"Which do you want first, the good news or the bad news?" Well, in the case of God's promise of hope in Jeremiah 29:11, God first gave His people some bad news. He informed the children of Israel they would remain in captivity away from their homeland for 70 years as punishment for repeatedly failing to follow His commands (verse 10).

But on the heels of the bad news came good news: At the end of their 70 years in exile, God would once again visit His people and fulfill His promise to return them to their land. This was great news of hope.

Seventy years is a l-o-n-g time! Imagine how easy it would be for the people to lose hope and assume that God had turned His back on them. Imagine how often they may have been tempted—perhaps daily!—to think that God no longer loved them or cared about them. But all such thoughts would definitely have been incorrect! To prevent such wrong thinking, God gave the Israelites this shining promise of hope through His prophet Jeremiah.

Oh, did Israel ever need to be encouraged! They needed to know that in spite of their situation they could still be firmly rooted in their trust in God and their belief in God's loving concern for them. Yes, they had sinned and disobeyed God repeatedly. But God was giving them *hope* that, even in the midst of their *calamity*, He was working out His *plans* for their lives and their *future*.

And God is working out His plan for your life as a couple as well. You, like the Israelites, can have confidence in God's plan for you, your marriage, and your endeavors. Why can you have such steadfast hope? Because your hope is not like a ship that is at the mercy of the changing winds. No, your hope is anchored in God Himself!

Because God has designed your personal couple agenda and is present with you, you can have boundless hope—a hope grounded in the promise of an all-powerful God. The stronger your faith in God is, the stronger your hope will be!

Lord, You alone are sovereign. Everything happens according to Your plan. Thank You that we can have confidence in Your guidance and provision…no matter what happens!

The Fountain of Life

Jim here!… One of the prized gifts my parents gave me as a child was an interest in reading. At an early age my mother enrolled me in a children's classics book club. Every month the mailman brought a new classic…and I was off again, sailing with pirates on wind-driven ships and exploring uncharted islands in search of hidden treasure (while Elizabeth was solving mysteries with Nancy Drew)!

One tale that particularly fascinated me was the story about the search for the fountain of youth—you know, the spring whose waters supposedly had the power to restore youth. Believing this legend, Juan Ponce de León, a Spanish explorer, set out in 1513 on an expedition from Puerto Rico to discover this fountain whose life-giving powers were said to originate from an island called Bimini.

Needless to say, Ponce de León did not find the fountain of youth. But he did discover a land mass on Easter Sunday of 1513. He named the new territory *Pascua Florida*, which is Spanish for "flower of Easter." Today we have this explorer to thank for naming the state of Florida for us.

This story of Juan Ponce de León points to the fascination people throughout time have had with life. Theirs is an obsession with life here and now and life in the hereafter. Such thoughts are constantly on every man and woman's mind, whether they verbalize it or not. Many ads on television offer new products that will make us look younger or feel more youthful. It appears people will spend almost any amount of money for "the fountain of youth." Yes, the preoccupation with life is permanently stamped on humanity.

But what if there was someone who could actually give you life? That would be terrific news, wouldn't it? Well, guess what: There *is* such a person, and His name is Jesus Christ. Listen to His promise:

> I have come that [you] may have life, and have it
> to the full (John 10:10 NIV).

Have the two of you ever talked about why Jesus, God in flesh, came to this earth? Well, His promise gives you and us His purpose. Jesus came to offer life—abundant life and eternal life. He also proclaimed, "I give eternal life to them, and they will never perish; and no one will snatch them out of My hand" (John 10:28 NASB). Jesus is a giver of life—abundant life, and a sustainer of life—eternal life.

And to whom did Jesus offer eternal life? To those sheep who *hear* His voice and *follow* His leading (John 10:3). Have you heard the voice of the Good Shepherd? If so, Jesus promises you will have life...and have it abundantly!

Thank You, Lord, for Your gift of eternal life. May we never allow the grind of daily life to distract us from the blessings You have so generously given us.

Nothing Can Separate

How often have you met a bona fide celebrity? Living in Southern California for almost 30 years, and working part of that time in Beverly Hills, gave me (Jim) a few opportunities to at least recognize several movie stars. I never actually met any of them, but it was a thrill to go home and play "Guess who I saw today?" with Elizabeth.

But both Elizabeth and I did meet a music celebrity in person several years ago at a dinner given by some friends. We never expected to meet such a celebrity because we're not in those kinds of social circles. This musician was Hal David, the writer of the words for *What the World Needs Now Is Love*. The music was composed by Burt Bacharach and sung by Jackie DeShannon.

Well, anyway, this songwriter was a very gracious and interesting man. It was fascinating to hear how he came to write the lyrics to this award-winning tune. And, as an added bonus that evening, the woman who sang the original release of this still-famous song was there with him. So, you guessed it! Our hosts asked these two "stars" to sing their well-known song! And before we realized what was happening, we—and everyone else in the entire restaurant— were all singing along with them. What a once-in-a-lifetime treat!

If you know the hit tune we're talking about, you are probably already humming along, right? And we bet you also agree with the message of the song. The world still needs love...of which there's still too little!

But note this powerful promise from God:

> God has not given us a spirit of timidity, but of power and love and discipline (2 Timothy 1:7 NASB).

Love is a vital biblical quality to possess. And for both men and women, it is also an attitude that is often misunderstood. Our society confuses love with lust. Lust is a strong physical and/or sexual desire. It can occur without any associated feelings of love or affection, becoming a one-way street to self-fulfillment and self-gratification.

God's kind of love, however, goes against all our normal tendencies. Unlike lust and self-gratification, God's kind of love is directed outwardly toward others. That's why God's promise of love—His kind of love—is so important for us to understand. That's also why such love will revolutionize your marriage. You must be careful not to confuse God's brand of love with what the world and our society would call love.

This Bible promise—"God has not given us a spirit of timidity, but of...love"—was given to a young preacher named Timothy. He was facing some pretty stiff opposition. Paul, his mentor, wrote to encourage Timothy to refuse to be intimidated and fearful. He was to remember that God had already given him a powerful resource that would combat his fear—love.

Timothy is not the only person to whom God gave this powerful promise. God has given *every* believer the resource of His divine love, and that includes us. His love "has been poured out within our hearts through the Holy Spirit" (Romans 5:5 NASB).

This promise of His eternal, inexhaustible, and ever-present love should be most comforting. As a couple, you have faced—

and you will face—hardships, persecution, illness, and ultimately, death. But these adversities should not cause you to be fearful nor ruin the quality of your life and marriage. Why? Because nothing (including these afflictions) "shall be able to separate us from the love of God which is in Christ Jesus our Lord" (Romans 8:39). Have no fear—God's love is near!

Father, even when affliction comes, may we rest in the assurance of Your ever-present love. Because Your love never runs out, ours is able to persevere no matter what life brings our way.

No Mistakes

We once met a woman to talk about some problems in her life that were not going away. As she spoke, her tale turned to her childhood and the extreme poverty and backwardness of her early home. It didn't take me long to see that this dear struggling woman was allowing these past circumstances, as difficult as they were, to affect her present situation...and was blaming God for both.

And this is common. Whenever tough times come our way, we can find ourselves falling into that same trap of thinking God made a mistake...that He wasn't there when we needed Him. Thoughts like these rob us of our hope.

The Bible, however, describes a God who is perfect in His wisdom, His ways, and His timing. He is a God who is with us always, and a God who loves us. During your tough times, you must turn to these biblical truths about God and let them comfort and assure you of His presence. In your trials and traumas, you must believe the Bible's teaching that God was and is with you always, that He doesn't make mistakes, and that He is always in control.

Through His inspired Word, God reminds you that He, the Divine Designer, knows what He is doing. He reveals that your history, whatever your experience, is not an error, but is in fact a part of His plan. And the result? Reminded that God is in control, you can then face life with hope in Him. And there's more good news! With this truth in mind, you don't need to use up your time and energy trying to reconcile some of the harsher aspects of reality (cancer, airplane crashes, incest, victims of drunk drivers). You can instead, by faith, and by His grace, acknowledge that...

> "For my thoughts are not your thoughts, neither are your ways my ways," declares the LORD. "As the heavens are higher than the earth, so are my ways higher than your ways and my thoughts than your thoughts" (Isaiah 55:8-9 NIV).

There has never been a mistake, and there never has been or ever will be even a split second when God is not present with you as a couple, superintending and being actively involved in your lives. Acknowledging that God has planned your path as a couple can help free you from bitterness and resentment toward people (including each other!), events, and circumstances. It also gives you hope! You become a hope-filled Christian couple when you remember—and grow to know—that God is the author of every moment of your married life.

Heavenly Father, whenever we are tempted to doubt Your love and faithfulness, may we remember that with You there are no mistakes. Help us to rest in Your perfect care.

The War Is Over!

At the close of the Pacific Theater of World War II, every Japanese soldier surrendered...except four: Lieutenant Hiroo Onoda and three of his men. Somehow Lieutenant Onoda and his group never received their superior officer's message to surrender. Therefore, the holdouts would not believe the war was over!

For the next three decades, Onoda and his men sought to avoid capture by the "enemy." In their minds, they were still at war. But slowly and surely, as the years passed by, one by one, the lieutenant's men were killed or surrendered...but not Onoda.

Can you imagine the shock this soldier's family must have felt when they were informed he was still alive? Onoda finally surrendered on March 9, 1974, at age 53—but only after his former commander met him and personally read the order that all combat activity was to cease. For Onoda, the war was over at last...30 years after it had ended!

Now let's talk about the two of you—about your lives, both together and as individuals. Have you received the official communiqué yet? Has someone come to you and relayed the message?

"What message?" you say.

The message that the war is over!

"What war?" you ask.

The war between God and sinners.

What a great message! God is no longer at war with you and us. We "sinners" can have peace with God. (And pardon us, but we're assuming that you consider yourselves to be sinners, too. Even the great apostle Paul confessed himself to be a sinner. In fact, he said, "I am the *worst*" of sinners—1 Timothy 1:15 NLT.)

But even though we are all sinners, God has made peace with us through His Son, the Lord Jesus Christ (Romans 5:1). The war *is* over. And because we are at *peace with God,* we can now enter into Jesus' powerful promise of the *peace of God:*

> Peace I leave with you, My peace I give to you (John 14:27).

Peace! A heart at rest. Serenity. This is what the whole world is looking for, isn't it? Now, the *worldly* kind of peace is defined as peace without conflict—*world peace.* But the *peace of God* is vastly different. The peace of God is tranquility…in any, all, and every circumstance.

Jesus offers you this kind of peace—His peace. He says, "Peace I leave with you, My peace I give to you." Yes, Jesus is offering you His peace—the peace of God. That's God's promise. But you can choose not to trust God. You can choose to continue to be anxious and worried. It's your choice. And, believe us, your choice will make a difference!

Lord, help us to choose peace over worry. Whenever we are uncertain about the future or our present problems, may we simply trust You and not our frail human "wisdom."

Never Apart

I was an only child (unlike Elizabeth, who grew up with three brothers). This had some great benefits for me. I didn't have to share my toys with any brothers or sisters. I also didn't have to share my parents' affection with other siblings. I was pretty much the center of attention. But there was one daily problem. I didn't have anyone to play with! So I was always trying to make friends and find playmates.

Very few people in this world like to be alone. And that's biblical! God created us, both male and female, to be social beings. God knew from the beginning of time that man needed companionship. It was God who noticed and said, "It is not good for the man to be alone; I will make him a helper suitable for him" (Genesis 2:18). And *voila*—it was done! God created Eve, gave her to Adam, and the two became the first married couple.

You have a partner-in-marriage. You probably also have his and her friends, as well as couple friends. And, as a member of a church, you have the body, other church members, to come alongside you in good times as well as in times of difficulty. But God promised His people over and over throughout the Bible that, regardless of whether they had any other person around them, they would still have Him—His presence—with them...at all times, no matter what was happening, where they were, or what they were facing.

God's promise of His presence applies to you as well. Jesus said,

> And surely I am with you always, to the very end
> of the age (Matthew 28:20 NIV).

That's the promise that we Christians can claim as individuals or as couples. God will be with you for as long as you live. And we all know none of us can make such a statement of our spouse. A spouse might die and leave, but God will always be present with us...even through such a hard time and its aftermath. What a powerful and comforting promise!

(Elizabeth here!...) The truth of God's presence especially brought me great comfort twice when I was apart from Jim. One time was when my scheduled flight home was suddenly rerouted due to a blizzard. There wasn't any way I could let Jim know what had happened. I remember sitting on that plane praying, "God, not one person in this world knows where I am." Then I remembered God's presence and added, "But You do!" His presence reassured me when I was "lost in space" and alone...or so I initially and erroneously thought!

The other time was when I underwent major surgery. I was wheeled into a preparation room, and Jim joined me. There he prayed for and with me. Jim was present for all the preliminaries, until finally the time came when I had to be rolled off to the surgery suite...and he wasn't allowed to go with me.

All I could do was lie there, helpless and praying, "Lord, yea, though I may be walking through the valley of the shadow of death (I don't know what the surgeon may find!), and yea, though I am entering the unknown (I had never had surgery before!), and yea, though I'm being put under with anesthetics (and may never wake up to see Jim again!), You are with me!"

And do you know what? He was…and He is! When your husband or wife cannot be with you, God can…and is!

Lord, thank You for Your constant presence in our lives. With You at our side, we have everything we need!

Riches in Glory

Many husbands—and wives too—suffer from ulcers, high blood pressure, heart problems, and a number of other illnesses due to the weight of the burden to provide financially for their families. The rigors of the demands on their jobs and their constant state of worry and anxiety take a daily toll. God's curse on Adam has definitely become a harsh reality, hasn't it? As God told Adam, "By the sweat of your face you will eat bread" (Genesis 3:19 NASB).

But there's good news! There is one kind of provision you as a couple never have to worry about, and that is God's provision for you. And with this good news comes the blessing of God's promised provision for your family as well (if and when that becomes a reality for the two of you).

Hidden in the writings of the apostle Paul is a powerful promise that sustained him every day of his life. And dear couple, it can sustain you, too! Here's the scene...

Paul is in jail (again!) for his faith. Heavy on his heart is his concern for his good friends in faraway Philippi. So Paul takes "pen" in hand and writes to his friends in Christ. In his letter he thanks these folks for a gift of financial support they had sent to him (Philippians 4:18). Then Paul, the master writer, uses the Philippians' provision for his needs as an illustration of how God will provide for their needs. For, you see, they were not a wealthy people—they gave to Paul out of "their extreme poverty" (2 Corinthians 8:2 NIV). What did Paul say to encourage these needy people?

> My God will meet all your needs according to the
> riches of his glory in Christ Jesus (Philippians 4:19 NIV).

Paul gave these poor Christians a promise of God's provision. And, the hope he passed on to them extends across the centuries to us.

And what will God provide for the two of you? Notice the promise: "My God will meet *all your needs*." Not your *wants*, but your *needs*. In other words, you can always count on God to supply all that is required to sustain your physical life.

And what are your needs? Jesus said that your heavenly Father knows what your needs are: What you need to *eat*...what you need to *drink*...what you need for *clothing* (Matthew 6:31-32). Pretty basic, isn't it? You can trust God to meet "all your needs."

It's impossible for you to comprehend God's "riches in glory"! They are boundless, limitless, infinite! And it was out of God's abundant storehouse that the Philippians' needs would be met. And, dear husband and wife, it is out of God's plentiful riches in glory that He provides for your needs, too.

And here's the backbone of this splendid promise: God provides *according to* His riches, not *out of* His riches. Do you see the difference? If God's supply was merely *out of His riches*, there would be a limit on His provision. His supply would have to be doled out, little by little. But no, our great, unlimited God takes care of us *according to His riches*—riches that are limitless. That means His provision for you is limitless...and so is God's promise.

In You, Lord, we have all we need. Thank You!

The Greatest Purpose

I'm sure you have heard stories of people who have survived incredible difficulties. Maybe you've even heard about those who have lived through the deprivations and inhumane treatment endured as prisoners-of-war. We, along with our family, had the sobering experience of touring Dachau, the infamous World War II concentration camp in Germany. One man's real-life survivor story of one of these camps is especially revealing and at the same time enlightening and educational.

Victor Frankl was an Austrian psychiatrist who spent years in a German concentration camp. Life in the camp was incredibly harsh and brutal. The prisoners were forced to work long hours, with little food, insufficient clothing, and inadequate shelter. As time dragged on, Frankl noticed that some of the prisoners collapsed under the pressure, gave up, and died, while others continued to stay alive under the same demands.

What made the difference? Using his psychiatric training, Dr. Frankl talked to the other inmates in the evenings. Over the months he noticed a pattern. Those prisoners who had something to live for, an objective that gave a sense of meaning to their lives or a purpose, were the ones who seemed to be able to mobilize their strength and survive.

As Frankl continued to interview his fellow prisoners, he found out that their objectives for living were individual and different. Each survivor had a focus and a passion that kept him alive. And Frankl was no exception. He had begun a book and had a fierce desire to survive and finish it. After the war, Victor Frankl completed what had motivated him to stay alive—his book!

Frankl's experience illustrates for you, for us, and for everyone the power of purpose. There is nothing as potent as a life lived with passion and purpose. And, we want to add, there is nothing as potent as a *marriage* that rallies around a marked purpose! The survivors in Frankl's concentration camp focused on a purpose that was personally inspired. In Frankl's case it was his book. Another man had a girlfriend he hoped to marry as soon as the war was over.

But what if you could have a purpose that wasn't inspired by our own desires? A purpose that came from a higher source— a divine source—from God? Wouldn't that be a grand purpose indeed? This brings us to yet another of God's powerful promises:

> Before I formed you in the womb I knew you,
> before you were born I set you apart; I appointed
> you... (Jeremiah 1:5 NIV).

God promised Jeremiah that he had a purpose. God had *appointed* Jeremiah as a prophet to the nations. Obviously that's not God's purpose for you today. But just as God promised Jeremiah a purpose, so He promises you a purpose. Do you know what God's promised purpose is? I hope you do. I am sure you can see that having a life-purpose, and especially God's purpose, has great significance.

Life makes little or no sense without an understanding that all roads lead back to God and His purposes (Romans 8:28). Without

God, your life has no meaning, and you have no hope (Ephesians 2:12). For meaning in life, look to your purpose.

Imagine the marriage in which each partner lives confidently, in which mutual energy is focused on a grand and compelling purpose, in which each mate encourages and promotes the other in living out his or her purpose. Now, that's *two* lives—and a marriage—with power and purpose! As God said (and as we've emphasized throughout this book), "Two are better than one" (Ecclesiastes 4:9).

Heavenly Father, You have a purpose for each or us. May we live in full yieldedness to You so that You can carry out Your purpose unhindered.

Rest

For almost 30 years we lived in the Los Angeles area. We loved it! And there's no doubt about it—Los Angeles is a city that never sleeps. It doesn't matter what time you are out and about. The roads, the streets, and the freeways are always packed with cars and people. But busyness and a hectic schedule are not unique to Los Angeles. Our New York son-in-law, Paul, leaves the house before daylight to catch a train into Manhattan and returns on that same train after dark. This dark-to-dark scenario is repeated for many people in almost every city around the world.

Whether we like it or not, or choose it or not, we are all members—or becoming members—of the "Busyness Club." As the pace of the world continues to pick up with faster travel, faster Internet access, faster computers (and don't forget fast food!), men, women, and even children(!) are finding less and less time to rest.

Every husband knows the pressure of providing for his wife and family. And in many cases, wives are working, too. Plus both husbands and wives must take the time to maintain a loving and caring relationship with their mates and with any children they have. For a Christian, there is the added stewardship of serving in some capacity at one's church. Fulfilling all these duties and obligations takes time—time that must be tacked onto an already jam-packed life.

How can we as married couples and individuals find help for this hectic life? This powerful promise provides the answer:

> Come to Me, all who are weary and heavy-laden,
> and I will give you rest (Matthew 11:28 NASB).

As a couple, we love this verse, and we imagine that you do, too. Just reading it causes us to exhale (whew!) and enjoy a measure of rest. What was it that moved Jesus to make this reassuring statement?

A quick answer is that the religious leaders of Jesus' day placed so many rules on the people that their "religion" had caused them to be "weary and heavy-laden." The people were weary from all of the rules and regulations that were impossible to fulfill. In short, they were worn out. Pleasing God seemed hopeless.

Enter Jesus! In this powerful promise, Jesus invited His audience—and each of us, too—to "Come to Me...and I will give you rest." His summons was to *come* participate in the promise of *rest*... which only He can *give*. Obviously, rest is supremely important to God. Therefore, it should be important to us to ensure that we rest our bodies, refresh our souls, and worship God. Remember, rest is part of God's plan.

In contrast to the religious leaders, Jesus offered mankind God's original design for rest to "all who are weary and heavy-laden." His rest included perfect fellowship and harmony with God. But there was one condition—God's offer of rest could become a reality only if and when the people heeded Jesus' invitation to "come to Me."

And dear friends, Jesus' offer of the gift of rest and refreshment is extended to you as well. God promises spiritual rest. His rest provides freedom from guilt over sin, deliverance from fear and despair, continued guidance and help from the Holy Spirit, and ultimate eternal rest.

There is no reason for either of you to continue to be "weary and heavy-laden" when you heed Christ's call to "come to Me." In Christ you will find relief and refreshment in a new relationship with God. Remember, rest is a gift of God.

Lord, so often we are weary. May we remember Your offer of rest— real rest. What a wonderful incentive for us to set aside alone time with You!

Time

It's true that our days are numbered. Indeed, they are in God's hands. He and He alone knows the length of our days on earth. In reality, then, that makes the minutes of a day all we have. That means, as the two age-old sayings go, "Today is all you have" and "There is no tomorrow." Jesus taught these truths in His parable of the rich fool who tore down his barns to build bigger ones. What did God say to this man? "Fool! This night your soul will be required of you" (Luke 12:20).

The on-purpose couple knows not to speak or think or act as if "today or tomorrow we will go to such and such a city" or do such and such a thing. Why? Because that couple knows the rest of the story:

> You do not even know what will happen tomorrow. What is your life? You are a mist that appears for a little while and then vanishes (James 4:14 NIV).

Today is all you have. Dear friends, each 24-hour portion that God chooses to give you is to be lived *in* Him, *unto* Him, *for* Him, *by* His strength, and with *His* plans in mind. Why? Because today *is* the future. Today is all you have to live out God's purposes. There is no guarantee of tomorrow.

But there's good news! The best thing about the future is that it comes only one day at a time. Today is all you have…but you do have today! That means today is the only day you have to live out God's purposes. How you manage today adds to the quality of the better life—and future—you are building. And hopefully, you are building your life and future purposefully and with God's glory in mind.

Each day when the two of you wake up, you must realize how blessed you are. Just think, the gift of a day—a whole, entire, precious and priceless day! But it's not *your* day. Oh, no—it's *God's* day! And you are a steward of it. Make it a habit to sit down at the calendar and pray together, "Lord, how do You want us to live this day? What is it You want us to do with this one day You have given us? What is the work You want us to accomplish today?"

This is how God's purposes are lived out in the present. Not a day is to be taken for granted. Not a day is to be wasted or frittered away. And every day is meant to count. What is it that makes a day count, and makes it count for a better life? Living it for God's purposes.

Knowing your purpose is a powerful motivating force. Make it a daily habit to reaffirm God's purposes for each of you and plan to live them out…just for today.

Every day we are alive comes from You, Lord. May we make each one count for You!

Strengthened

One evening we were flipping through the television channels when we discovered the Power Team. We had heard about these big guys before but had never watched their show. So we paused for a moment to get a better understanding of their outreach ministry.

In case you haven't heard of the Power Team, they are a group of ex-jocks and body-builder types who tour the country and share their testimonies about what it means to have faith in Jesus Christ. These guys are incredible! They can break huge blocks of concrete with their bare hands, just to name one of their feats of strength. They are a team of Christian men who use their physical strength to entertain and speak about their love for Jesus.

But these men are not the only ones who can be on a "power team." If the two of you know and love Jesus, you too can be assured of God's promise of strength and power. Where can you get some of this strength, you ask? Here's the answer...and a promise for your team of two:

> I can do all things through Christ who strengthens
> me (Philippians 4:13).

Now, let us quickly state that when you and your sweetie appropriate this promise of God's strength, you won't be able to break huge blocks of concrete! But God's kind of strength will allow you to be victorious in all areas of living the Christian life…and the Christian *married* life. That's better than breaking concrete blocks, don't you think?

"I can do all things through Christ who strengthens me." The triumphant words of this promise come from the apostle Paul, and his confident reference to "all things" has to do with being in control in every circumstance. So, whether Paul had a lot or a little, or whether he suffered a lot or a little, he was able to handle it, whatever "it" was. His attitude of "I can do all things" was the same in every circumstance (see Philippians 3:12).

Do you have any issues, any problems, any lacks, any "its" and "things" to deal with in your lives and your marriage? Then read on as Paul tells you how he made it through "all things."

The promise—The first half of this familiar verse declares a truth: "I can do all things," or "I can do everything" (NIV). This is the kind of message that you would expect to hear from a motivational speaker or a coach. It conveys the idea of self-reliance and self-assurance. It says, "*You* can do it! *You* can do anything you want to do if you put your mind to it."

Statements like these may be true in some areas of a person's life. Sure, given enough determination and willpower, you *can* accomplish a lot in life. But that's not what this verse is saying, when you consider the *source* of such power. So you must read on and finish Paul's message. He reveals that you "can do all things *through Christ*" who strengthens you!

The source—Friends, *Christ* is the source of our strength. Don't miss it—it's *Christ! He* is the reason we can do *all things* in the spiritual realm. How was Paul able to have this kind of optimistic perspective on the issues of life? It was because of Christ.

How often have you tried to live some aspect of your life in your own strength and ability? You had the skills. You had the know-how. Maybe the two of you even had the money. But you tried to go it alone, without considering the Lord, to do it yourself. Well, how did you do?

We can make a pretty good guess, because we've been there and done that too! We're guessing you probably failed miserably. So the message is loud and clear—to become a "power couple" you must stop trusting in your own strength and abilities and instead rely on Christ and His strength.

Father, when we catch ourselves relying on our own strength, may we immediately turn our full dependence upon You. Through You, we can do all things.

A Little Perspective

Leo Tolstoy is one of the world's most renowned authors. Almost everyone has heard of his novel *War and Peace,* which was published in 1886. Tolstoy was born into a privileged aristocratic family, so he didn't have to worry about survival like most other children did in nineteeth-century Russia.

But Tolstoy did have his personal struggles as a child and an adolescent. He wrestled with what most young boys and girls and many adults struggle with in our day and age—a sense of worth. Because of his low personal estimation of his physical appearance, Tolstoy at one point in his life begged God to work a miracle and transform him into a handsome man. (Sounds a lot like the kind of request many people would make today, doesn't it?)

Not until years later, as an adult, did Tolstoy realize that external looks are not what gives a person worth. In some of his writings, Tolstoy revealed his discovery that inner beauty and a strong character are what pleases God the most.

Once Tolstoy's mind and heart came to recognize what is truly important in life, his writings evidenced a new sense of passion and purpose. His characters took on a more courageous and confident nature, a reflection of Tolstoy's new personal confidence.

Like Tolstoy, many men and women today suffer from what has been labeled by some as low self-esteem or low self-image. In their minds, there is something wrong with them. They are too tall…too short…too large…too whatever. Some who fail to understand their worth handle it by withdrawing into a shell of sadness and loneliness. Others try to compensate in some other way, such as putting on a mask of self-assurance—a boisterous, loud, life-of-the-party facade. It is no wonder that so many folks have problems with self-respect when they place their entire focus on "self"!

But what if you were to take a different perspective and talk about your worth in God's eyes? Or your worth in Jesus Christ? Here's God's answer to the self-esteem problem as given in this powerful promise from Jesus:

> Are not two sparrows sold for a penny? Yet not one of them will fall to the ground outside your Father's care. And even the very hairs of your head are all numbered. So don't be afraid; you are worth more than many sparrows (Matthew 10:29-31 NIV).

When Jesus declared this comforting statement, He was assuring His disciples that whatever might happen in the future as they preached the gospel, they could be courageous and confident. Why? Because of their worth to the Father and His concern for them.

Jesus masterfully drove His point home: Even when a single, seemingly insignificant sparrow falls to the ground, it does not happen "outside your Father's care." Jesus reasoned that if God is this concerned about *one* sparrow, how much more do you think He is concerned about the two of you? And the answer? More! Much more! Jesus said "you are worth more than many sparrows." Never doubt your God-given worth and your significance to Him!

Lord, how great is Your love for us! And how wonderful that it is unending.

DAY TWENTY-SIX

Worrywart

The weather had finally cleared. It had been an awful winter! Storm after storm had dumped a record amount of snow on the friendly suburb where Sue Higgins lived. But on this day the weather had turned warm and sunny. You would think the bright, cheery day would have raised Sue's spirits, but not so. The black cloud of worry that shadowed Sue's life wasn't about to go away.

The last few years had been a financial roller coaster for the Higgins family. Bill, Sue's husband, was in middle management at the main office of a major automobile plant. There had been some previous scares, but Bill had managed to hang on to his position. But yesterday the company had announced a cutback of 8000 jobs at the plant. To make matters worse, they were *still* trying to pay off the credit card debt that had mounted up during their last vacation. Sue's financial situation seemed hopeless.

Have you sensed the heart-pounding fear that Sue experienced as she suffered and worried in the area of finances? Her story strikes home in far too many places. No doubt you too have had your bouts with killer trials in the financial realm! And even now you may still wake up in the night with your stomachs churning and your minds running wild, tempted to wonder and worry about not only the present but the future.

Since Adam and Eve were forced out of the Garden of Eden (Genesis 3), mankind has faced the problem of finding and providing food, clothing, and shelter on a daily basis. Provision is a basic, practical area of life and existence. And it's a common— and daily—cause for worry. To have food takes money. To have clothes involves money. And to have shelter requires money. For most people, money comes from having a job, whether that job is done in a place of business, on a farm, or at home.

But Jesus instructs us clearly regarding worry about these basic elements of life. He told His followers,

> Do not worry about your life, what you will eat
> or drink; or about your body, what you will wear
> (Matthew 6:25 NIV).

Jesus' message is crystal clear. It can't be missed or misinterpreted. His followers were worrying about the basics of daily living. They were fretting about food and clothes—so much so that they were losing their focus on God, on one hundred percent devotion to Him and living out His kingdom priorities. Their service to God (which is eternal) was diluted and at risk due to their obsession with daily basics (which are temporal and earthly).

It's a fact that fear and worry can immobilize you in your kingdom work. They distract you from your worship and love of God. And your service to God and His people is hampered and blocked when you worry about yourselves and fail to trust Him. Today, make the choice as a couple to give all your worries over to God!

Heavenly Father, You tell us not to worry. May we cast all our cares upon You right now!

Your Treasure

When we were first married, we wanted many of the same things everyone wants. We wanted good jobs, a good income, a new car, and an exciting lifestyle—with, of course, the funds to finance them. As time went by and we obtained these goals, we began to wish for a terrific home to own, decorate, and fill with brand-new designer furniture. Within eight years of marriage, we had all this. And because Jim received many raises and promotions and bonuses, we had a stock portfolio and a large savings account. Life was good.

But then what? There we were, stuffing our lives full of stuff, and still we were restless. So we traveled. We camped. We took night classes. We joined a sailing club. We developed hobbies like photography, bicycling, and woodworking. We regularly read every book published that made the *New York Times* bestseller list. We played chess and belonged to a competitive bridge club.

Still we couldn't shake the emptiness. As hard as we tried, and as much money as we earned and spent, and as many things as we stockpiled and owned, we still searched for something more. But nothing lasted and nothing satisfied...and we weren't even 30 years old.

Well, praise God for His intervention in our lives. By His grace we gladly stepped into a new life, a life where there are never any voids—a life filled with Jesus Christ and goals centered around eternity and eternal values. It wasn't long before Jim resigned from his job to go back to school to prepare for ministry. We sold our home and most of the furniture and moved into a very small and much older home that had nothing but the basics. Later in life our financial position did stabilize, but our perspective on our possessions was permanently altered.

Because of the temporary nature of our possessions, Jesus tells us exactly where we should place our focus.

> But lay up for yourselves treasures in heaven, where neither moth nor rust destroys and where thieves do not break in and steal. For where your treasure is, there your heart will be also (Matthew 6:20-21).

Where is your focus? Where is your "treasure"? Put another way, what occupies your thoughts and time? The goal is to make sure your first loyalties—your priority heart commitments—are on the right things, the things that cannot fade away, the things that can never be stolen, the things that cannot wear out (and are never out of fashion!). In short, the things that last—the things that are eternal.

Lord, may we look at our treasures with clear eyes that can discern the temporary from the eternal. May we pursue those treasures that will last forever!

Taking Control

Just like you, we sometimes need help with discipline…every day of our lives! From the first decision of the morning in answer to the sound of the alarm clock (Will I respond or not? Will I get up or hit the snooze button?) to the final decision at day's end (Will I read a little longer, work a little longer, watch television a little longer, or will I turn out the light and get to sleep so I can get up when the alarm goes off?), we all need discipline.

No one has to tell you that discipline in every area of life is crucial. You already know that discipline is important for what it produces in you—spiritual growth, personal accomplishment, and physical well-being…in other words, a better life. But discipline is also important for what it produces in you that is seen by others, which in turn can produce change in them. You can be a motivating model and an example. And whether you like it or not, others are watching you. Your life and marriage have a positive or negative effect on everyone you live with, know, or encounter.

And yet, no matter how disciplined (or undisciplined!) you already are, there's always room for growth. There's always another area the two of you can together decide to tackle and improve.

There's always something to learn, try, and perfect…a small change to make or a new step to take.

Self-control and self-discipline are manifestations of God's Spirit at work in us (Galatians 5:22-23). Paul also reminds us,

> So I say, walk by the Spirit, and you will not grat-
> ify the desires of the flesh (Galatians 5:16 NIV).

If you are walking by the Spirit—if you're seeking to live your life according to His plan—you will exhibit self-control. This word literally means to be the master of oneself. Picture wrapping your arms around yourself and grasping onto yourself and holding yourself in restraint. That's self-control. Try that the next time you have a desire to overindulge in some area. And remember…character does not reach its best until it is controlled, harnessed, and disciplined.

It helps to understand that self-control is energized by the power of the Holy Spirit in you. As you and your spouse walk by the Spirit, He gives you the ability to overcome the temptations of the flesh (Galatians 5:16). But sin and disobedience grieve the Holy Spirit of God and quench the Spirit and His power to help you in your fight against sin (Ephesians 4:30 and 1 Thessalonians 5:19). So if you want to experience self-discipline, you must keep a short account with God. Quickly confess your sins—any of them and all of them. The result of this one step is a victorious life of Christian discipline, a life of power and beauty, a better life.

Lord, our heart's desire is to have a positive influence on others. Help us to recognize where we need greater discipline…so that others are blessed and You are honored.

A Different Perspective

When Jim and I first married, we lived on a honeymooner's budget, which means we did most of our furniture shopping at the local flea market. One day we discovered a wonderful antique brass bed. Orangey and almost black from the oxidation of the metal, its dismantled pieces leaned against the wall of a dingy booth behind other sparkling, more desirable items. But the price was right for us.

That old bed instantly became a treasure to us. But it had to be cleaned before we could use it and be proud of it. So we hauled our find home, set it up, and Jim went to work on it to see what he could do about the discoloration. When I checked on his progress, I was alarmed that he hadn't taken a soft cloth and polish to the brass bed. No, he was laboring away with steel wool and caustic cleanser! And he rubbed...and rubbed...and rubbed. And the harder he rubbed, the brighter the brass shone. It came alive and was even more outstanding than we'd dreamed!

God's testing of you through trials has a similar effect on your faith in Him. His trials are good for you. They bring out the best in you. They prove what you are made of and what you've learned—or not learned—as Christians. They reveal how you've grown—or not grown. These tests are your vigorous "rubbing" by God. So you need to see God's involvement in your life, as hard or difficult as it may be at the time, as a positive. That is possible because His tests contribute to your becoming stable—rocklike in character, solid and true, able to endure whatever comes your way.

Faith is constant when circumstances are good. But when times are adverse your faith in God is exercised and surges. As the saying goes, "Adversity is God's university." It is His teaching tool. And tested faith results in tested character. Testing teaches you how to use your mind to think and view life and its difficulties through God's eyes, through His perspective, which will almost always be vastly different from yours. He declares,

> My thoughts are not your thoughts, nor are your
> ways My ways (Isaiah 55:8 NASB).

As you as a couple gain self-control and operate your lives and marriage from the rock of faith, your wild emotions will be tamed.

Yes, oftentimes you don't understand the reasons for the tests and what they accomplish. You perceive them as negative and painful. But remember that old brass bed...and how it shone after some muscle work. Welcome the tests God sends your way. That way you'll shine as trophies of His grace!

Lord, we trust You as a loving heavenly Father who desires the best for His children. Help us to be willing recipients of whatever trials You know will help us grow spiritually strong.

The Maze

Imagine a maze in an English garden. These intriguing puzzles, created by six- or seven-foot hedges, were used initially to provide people with some entertaining exercise after their meals. The diners would enter the confusing and baffling network of shrubs and try to find their way to the pleasant place in the center of the maze where there was usually a tree, some flowering plants, and a garden seat where they could sit, relax, and visit…before trying to find their way out.

That's exactly the way life is! You follow along the maze of life, randomly making turns and choosing your path. Then you come to know Christ as your Lord and Savior. From that point on, you have purpose—to serve God. You're still traversing the maze of life, but now you have direction. God keeps you moving forward as you pray and dedicate your life to serving Him, becoming more Christlike, and spreading the gospel. As you begin to grow and move along in your Christian life, you come to corners…special moments when God guides your life into new directions or deeper understandings of His purpose for you. And off you go, following God's will on the new path! Unfortunately, sometimes you stray from God's will or misunderstand His direction or come to dead

246   A Couple After God's Own Heart

ends. Then, through further prayer, you take action and seek the Lord for clarification or new guidance…and set off accordingly.

While you're in the maze, you never know who or what you'll encounter. You don't even know exactly where you're going! But you do know that you are to keep moving. And as you continue on according to God's will and His leading, He fulfills His purpose for you. God doesn't ask you to understand the twists and turns, the whys and the hows of life. He asks only that you trust that He is working His purpose in you as you live out your purpose of serving Him!

> And we know that in all things God works for the good of those who love him, who have been called according to his purpose (Romans 8:28 NIV).

How thrilling it is to know God has a purpose for you and your marriage. That's yet another sparkling reason why you can have joy and hope in Him each day…no matter what happens in those 24 hours. Praise Him for His abundant grace, His constant provision, and His unending care over your marriage!

Father, we are deeply grateful You brought us together into this wonderful relationship called marriage. Our prayer is that others will see Your wisdom, love, and grace in us as we yield ourselves fully to whatever You desire to do in our lives.

Notes

1. Norman H. Wright, *Communication: Key to Your Marriage* (Ventura, CA: Gospel Light, 2000).

2. Michael Kendrick and Daryl Lucas, eds., *365 Life Lessons from Bible People—A Life Application Devotional* (Wheaton, IL: Tyndale House, 1996), Life Lesson 1.

3. These five levels of communication are adapted from John Powell, *Why Am I Afraid to Tell You Who I Am?* 2d ed. (Allen, TX: Thomas More Association; March 1990).

4. Romans 4; Galatians 3:6-29; Hebrews 11:8-12; James 2:21-23.

5. Donald Cole, *Abraham, God's Man of Faith* (Chicago: Moody Press, 1977).

6. See Genesis 2:18; Ephesians 5:22, 33; Titus 2:4.

7. See Genesis 28:10-22; 32:24-30; 35:9-15.

8. Richard L. Strauss, *Living in Love* (Wheaton, IL: Tyndale House, 1978), p. 46.

9. The Williams translation—Curtis Vaughn, gen. ed., *The New Testament from 26 Translations* (Grand Rapids, MI: Zondervan Publishing House, 1967), p. 901.

10. Herbert Lockyer, *The Women of the Bible* (Grand Rapids, MI: Zondervan , 1975), p. 185.

11. Lockyer, p. 34.

12. Ronald F. Youngblood, "1, 2 Samuel," in *The Expositor's Bible Commentary*, vol. 3, ed. Frank E. Gaebelein (Grand Rapids, MI: Zondervan, 1992), p. 949.

13. Lockyer, p. 36.

14. Bruce B. Barton, et al, *Life Application Bible Commentary—Romans* (Wheaton, IL: Tyndale House, 1992), p. 289.

Other Great Books by Jim and Elizabeth George

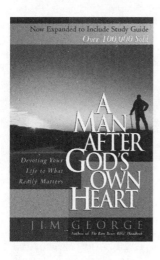

A Man After God's Own Heart

Jim George

More than 100,000 copies sold!

Many Christian men want to be men after God's own heart... but how do they do this? Jim George shows that a heartfelt desire to practice God's priorities is all that's needed.

You will find encouragement and learn how to:

- gain respect by modeling integrity at your job
- enjoy greater intimacy with God
- powerfully shape the hearts of your children
- draw your wife closer by serving and honoring her
- possess the spiritual strength to defend against temptation

Embark with Jim on a spiritual journey toward greater growth and maturity...and make giant strides toward becoming a man after God's own heart. Includes a study guide great for group and individual study.

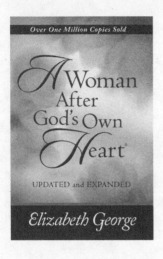

A Woman After God's Own Heart®

Elizabeth George

More than 1,000,000 copies sold!

A *Woman After God's Own Heart®* is Elizabeth George's flagship book with over 1,000,000 copies sold. This popular bestseller is filled with rich advice, spiritual wisdom, and practical application. Elizabeth shares how a woman can follow God and seek His heart in every area of her life. Her warm insights will help you...

- simplify your life by focusing on God's priorities
- build a stronger marriage and friendships by being an encourager
- respond to circumstances with confidence by seeing yourself through God's loving eyes
- make wise choices and teach your children how to do the same

Let God fulfill His greatest desire for you. Allow Him to transform you by preparing your heart and mind to embrace His incredible work. You will find lasting joy and peace in a life of prayer, in a life of priorities, and in a life as *A Woman After God's Own Heart*.

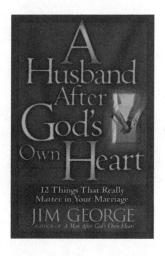

A Husband After God's Own Heart

Jim George

The closer a husband is to God, the closer he will grow to his wife. That's why it's so vital for husbands to pursue God's heart and get to know His perfect design for the man's role in the marriage relationship. Jim George will help you build a richer and deeper marriage as you discover how to...

- win your wife's heart through loving leadership
- build a happier home through wise guidance
- enjoy better communication through careful listening
- increase your family's spiritual growth by example
- excel at your job without sacrificing family priorities

Jim addresses 12 areas of a husband's life, providing men with practical applications for becoming a husband after God's own heart.

This book includes a helpful study guide and makes a powerful resource for men's Sunday school classes, small group studies, and a wonderful gift for engaged couples and new husbands.

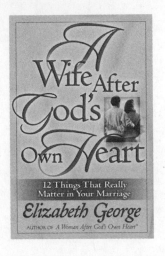

A Wife After God's Own Heart

Elizabeth George

What does it take to have a great marriage? Becoming a wife after God's own heart may sound difficult and downright challenging. But it doesn't have to be. Bestselling author Elizabeth George reveals what the Bible really says about how to have an exceptional marriage. With step-by-step guidance, she will help you...

- feel more confident as a wife
- communicate more effectively
- become a better team player
- have more fun in your marriage
- improve sexual intimacy with your husband

A Wife After God's Own Heart reveals how you can have what every married woman desires—a wonderful marriage filled with mutual love, friendship, romance, and happiness. As an added bonus, each chapter ends with "little things" you can do today to enhance your relationship with your husband.

This book makes a powerful resource for women's Sunday school classes, small group studies, and makes a great gift for engaged couples and new wives.

Books by Elizabeth George

- Beautiful in God's Eyes
- Breaking the Worry Habit...Forever
- Embracing God's Grace Finding God's Path through Your Trials
- Finding God's Path Through Your Trials
- Following God with All Your Heart
- The Heart of a Woman Who Prays
- Life Management for Busy Women
- Loving God with All Your Mind
- Loving God with All Your Mind DVD and Workbook
- A Mom After God's Own Heart
- A Mom After God's Own Heart Devotional
- Moments of Grace for a Women's Heart
- Quiet Confidence for a Woman's Heart
- Raising a Daughter After God's Own Heart
- The Remarkable Women of the Bible
- Small Changes for a Better Life
- Walking With the Women of the Bible
- A Woman After God's Own Heart®
- A Woman After God's Own Heart® Deluxe Edition
- A Woman After God's Own Heart®— Daily Devotional
- A Woman's Daily Walk with God
- A Woman's Guide to Making Right Choices
- A Woman's High Calling
- A Woman's Walk with God
- A Woman Who Reflects the Heart of Jesus
- A Young Woman After God's Own Heart
- A Young Woman After God's Own Heart— A Devotional
- A Young Woman's Guide to Prayer
- A Young Woman's Guide to Making Right Choices

Study Guides

- Beautiful in God's Eyes Growth & Study Guide
- Finding God's Path Through Your Trials Growth & Study Guide
- Following God with All Your Heart Growth & Study Guide
- Life Management for Busy Women Growth & Study Guide
- Loving God with All Your Mind Growth & Study Guide
- Loving God with All Your Mind Interactive Workbook
- A Mom After God's Own Heart Growth & Study Guide
- The Remarkable Women of the Bible Growth & Study Guide
- Small Changes for a Better Life Growth & Study Guide
- A Wife After God's Own Heart Growth & Study Guide
- A Woman After God's Own Heart® Growth & Study Guide
- A Woman's Call to Prayer Growth & Study Guide
- A Woman's High Calling Growth & Study Guide
- A Woman Who Reflects the Heart of Jesus Growth & Study Guide

Children's Books

- A Girl After God's Own Heart
- A Girl After God's Own Heart Devotional
- God's Wisdom for Little Girls
- A Little Girl After God's Own Heart

Books by Jim George

- 10 Minutes to Knowing the Men and Women of the Bible
- The Bare Bones Bible® Handbook
- The Bare Bones Bible® for Teens
- A Boy After God's Own Heart
- A Husband After God's Own Heart
- Know Your Bible from A to Z
- A Leader After God's Own Heart
- A Man After God's Own Heart
- A Man After God's Own Heart Devotional
- The Man Who Makes a Difference
- A Young Man After God's Own Heart
- A Young Man's Guide to Making Right Choices

Books by Jim & Elizabeth George

- A Couple After God's Own Heart
- A Couple After God's Own Heart Interactive Workbook
- God's Wisdom for Little Boys
- A Little Boy After God's Own Heart

About the Authors

Jim and Elizabeth George are bestselling authors, with a combined 8 million books in print, including *A Man After God's Own Heart* and *A Woman After God's Own Heart*.®

For information about Jim and Elizabeth, their books, and their ministries, and to sign up for their newsletters or join them on Facebook and Twitter, visit their websites:

www.ElizabethGeorge.com
www.JimGeorge.com